PRAYER STORM

DAILY PRAYER GUIDE

BE DILIGENT!

MAY – JUNE 2025

Godson T. Nembo

CRNPUBLICATIONS   IEM PRESS

BE DILIGENT!

Copyright @ April 2025

Published in Cameroon by:
Christian Restoration Network
crnprayerstorm@gmail.com,
prayerstorm@christianrestorationnetwork.org

ISBN: 978-1-63603-308-2

CONTACT
P.O. Box 31339 Biyem-assi, Yaounde, Cameroon
Tel.: 679.46.57.17, 652.38.26.93 or 696.56.58.64
Email: **godsonnembo@gmail.com** or
contact@christianrestorationnetwork.org
www.christianrestorationnetwork.org

WHERE TO BUY THIS PRAYER GUIDE:
SEE THE LAST PAGE

YOU CAN ACCESS ALL PRINTED HARD COPIES
OF OUR BOOKS FOR ANY SPECIFIED
DURATION AT YOUR DOORSTEP.
Contact (237) 679465717 for subscription and payment
details.

Prayer Storm Online Store: With MTN or Orange
Mobile Money *(for those in Cameroon)* and E-Wallet *(for those
abroad)*, you can easily obtain the electronic version of this
book and other CRN publications via **www.amazon.com**
at **https://shorturl.at/pqxyT** or
www.christianrestorationnetwork.org/our-bookstore
or **https://goo.gl/ktf3rT**

Printed in Yaounde, Cameroon by Mama press: (237)
677581523

TESTIMONIES:
Your testimony is a weapon against the kingdom of
darkness. It is also a seed for someone else's miracle. Share
with us what God has used this prayer guide and our books
to do in your life; by SMS, telephone call or email.

BECOME A MINISTRY PARTNER:
Call the numbers: (237) 679.46.57.17 or 652.38.26.93 or
696.56.58.64 or send an email to:
crnprayerstorm@gmail.com or
contact@christianrestorationnetwork.org

Send your financial seed to:

- ECOBANK Acc. Nº: **0040812604565101**
- Carmel Cooperative Credit Union Ltd. Bamenda Acc. Nº: **261**
- ORANGE Mobile Money Acc. Nº: **699902618**
- MTN Mobile Money Acc. Nº: **674495895**

A NEED FOR DISTRIBUTORS:

If you are interested in the distribution of this Prayer Storm Daily Prayer Guide, call or send an SMS to any of these numbers for negotiations: (237) 675.68.60.05 or 677.43.69.64 or 652.38.26.93 or 696.56.58.64 or send an email to: **crnprayerstorm@gmail.com** (see last page).

TABLE OF CONTENTS

IMPORTANT EVENTS/ANNOUNCEMENTS

SPECIAL PRAYER PROGRAM			
	Venue	**Theme**	*From Thursday 3rd to Saturday 5th July 2025*
RESTORA TION PRAYER CAMP 9th **Edition**	Salle des fêtes « FONTAINE DE GRACE » at Montée Jouvence Yaounde, Cameroon	*DEEP DELIVE RANCE*	
Register immediately online via https://forms.gle/r1uM3UhNNQrmRFb19. WhatsApp Contact: (237) 681722404 or 679465717/ Call: (237) 695722340 or 652382693.			

SPECIAL PROGRAM: I PRAY FOR YOU

Join Pastor Godson for a half hour morning devotion
every **MONDAY, WEDNESDAY, and FRIDAY**
from **6am** live on Facebook, YouTube
@PastorGodsonNemboTangumonkem

HOUR OF RESTORATION

Join Pastor Godson & Anna TANGUMONKEM for
HOUR OF RESTORATION **every TUESDAY** morning
from **6 – 7:30am** in the banquet hall: Salle des
fêtes « Fontaine de grâce » at Jouvence, Mendong street –
Yaounde, Cameroon..
A time of prophetic intercession for individuals, families and the nations.

ANNOUNCEMENTS

➤ Festival of Fire series No. 1-4 and Power Must Change Hands Vol. 1-10 now available at XAF 3,000. Send your orders from today.

➤ Annual subscription to the Daily Prayer Guide from XAF 10,000 for electronic copies.

➤ All our books are available at our Head office located at Carrefour Biyem-Assi, third floor in the storey building, opposite Campus Crusade for Christ. **Contact:** 681.72.24.04, 695.72.23.40.

➤ Prayer Storm Bookshop at Cow Street Nkwen – Bamenda sells our books, Bibles and excellent Christian literature. **Contact:** 675.14.04.50, 674.59.35.98, 679.46.57.17.

"RESTORATION CAMP" Project

• The project for the establishment of the base for CRN in Yaounde, Cameroon began in January 2020.

• The LAYING OF THE FOUNDATION STONE FOR THE RESTORATION PRAYER HOUSE at Tsinga Village, Yaounde, took place in December 2023.

• For information on how to be part of the project, call or send SMS to **(237) 674.49.58.95, 678.16.46.88, 673.50.42.33, 699.90.26.18.**

Feedback Questionnaire:

We will love to hear your suggestions on how we can improve on this book: Send your comments to **(237) 681722404**, use the link https://prayer-stormdevotional.paperform.com/ or scan the QR CODE shown here to fill the online form.

HOW TO BECOME A CHILD OF GOD

Going to church and praying is not enough. *"Except a man is BORN AGAIN, he CANNOT SEE the kingdom of God." (John 3:3)*.

The following steps will help you know how you can be born again.

Step 1: God Loves You and Offers a Wonderful Plan for Your Life

"For God so loved the world that He gave His only begotten Son, that whoever believes in Him should not perish but have everlasting life" (John 3:16). Jesus said, *"I came that they might have life and have it to the full." (John 10:10)*.

No matter who you are and what you have done, God still loves you and wants to save you (Rom.5:8).

Step 2: Your Sins Have Separated You from God; That Is Why You Are Not Experiencing His Wonderful Plan for Your Life

"For all have sinned and fall short of the glory of God" (Rom.3:23)
"The wages of sin is death (spiritual separation from God) Rom.6:23.

All your religious activities and efforts cannot save you. God has provided a solution for you.

Step 3: Jesus Christ Is the Only Way Back to God

Jesus said, *"I am the way, the truth and the life, No one comes to the father except through me" (John 14:6)*. Jesus is the only sacrifice God can accept for your sins. Through Him you can connect to God's plan for your life.

Step 4: You Must Personally Receive Jesus Christ as Your Saviour and Lord. Then You Can Know and Experience God's Plan for Your Life

Receive Him by personal invitation and by faith. *"Behold, I stand at the door and knock. If anyone hears My voice and opens the door (your heart), I will come in to him and dine with him, and he with Me." (Rev.3:20).*

If you are ready now to give your life to Jesus Christ, pray this prayer with all your heart.

"Dear Lord Jesus Christ, I need you. I open the door of my life and receive you as my Saviour and Lord. Forgive all my sins and wash me with your blood. Make me the kind of person you want me to be. Thank you for saving me."

Congrats! You are now a child of God.

Call us now let us pray for you: (237) 652.38.26.93 or 696.56.58.64

(Pastor Godson T. Nembo & Prayer Storm Team)

NOW THAT YOU ARE BORN AGAIN

Making the decision to become a born-again Christian, is the best decision you've ever made in your entire life and I congratulate you for that. The following points will help you enjoy your newfound life in Christ Jesus.

1. **Live with the Consciousness that You are Saved:** It is fundamental that you are certain of your new faith. This is referred to as the Assurance of Salvation. Believe that your sins have been forgiven and forgotten by God because of the price Jesus paid by His sacrificial death on the cross and that you are no longer under any condemnation (Acts 16:31, Rom.8:1-2, 2Cor.5:17, Jn.1:12).

2. **Join a Fellowship:** By new birth, you have entered the family of God. Locate a church that teaches and practises the scriptures truthfully, where the worship enables you to encounter God, and where the people are friendly and spiritual growth is encouraged (Heb.10:25, Gal.6:10).

3. **Get a Bible and Study It Daily:** You can begin from John, then Acts, Romans, etc. Just as a baby needs physical nourishment in order to grow, the Word of God is also the spiritual food by which we grow into Christlikeness (1Pet.2:2, Jn.5:24). Consult other mature Christians for any explanations.

4. **Commune Daily with God:** Through prayer, we talk with God, express our burdens to Him, as well as offer worship, praise and appreciation. We also have the

privilege to get God speak to us, showering upon us His love, peace, blessings and divine direction (Rom.10:9, 1Thess.5:17, 1Pet.5:8).

5. **Destroy Satan's Property in Your Keeping:** Desist from anything that does not glorify God. Do away with anything evil related to your sinful past, such as pornographic materials, stolen money and possessions, talismans, charms, juju, etc. (2Cor.6:17, Tit.2:11).

6. **Separate from Evil Friends and Get New Godly Friends:** Now that you are born again, you must discontinue the former way of life and walk in the truth (Ps.1:1-3, 2Cor.4:2; 5:17, Eph.4:22, 1Jn.1:6).

7. **Get Baptized:** Water baptism by immersion publicly authenticates our salvation and affirms our membership in the body of Christ (Rom.6:4, Col.2:12, Matt.28:19, Acts 2:38, 8:36).

8. **Seek the Baptism of the Holy Spirit:** The Holy Spirit assures us that we are saved and empowers us to live a holy life and do exploits for God through special gifts (Rom.8:14, Acts 2:1-4; 10:38, Eph.5:18).

9. **Tell Others about Jesus:** Our character should testify about our inner transformation. Also, our eagerness to tell others about God's love and lead them to Christ is also evidential about our salvation (Jn.4:28-29, Acts 4:10; 22:14, 2Tim.2:2).

10. **Worship God with Your Wealth through Offerings and Tithes:** Our cheerful giving is essential in

advancing God's Kingdom – freewill offerings and tithe (one-tenth
of our increase) (Deut.16:16-17, Prov.3:9-10, 2Cor:9:7).

11. **Make the Life of Christ Your Standard:** Fix your eyes on Jesus, the Author and Finisher of our faith Make Him your Role Model (Heb.12:2, Phil.2:5-11, Eph.4:24).

12. **Don't Abandon; Rise and Continue, if you Fall:** The Christian race may seem tough and challenging, with persecutions, distractions, oppositions, and even discouragements. But rest assured, you will make it by faith (Prov.24:16, Isa.41:10, Phil.1:6).

I pray that you will stand firm, and finish well like other heroes of faith, in Jesus' name! Amen.

Call us for counselling and prayer: (237) 652.38.26.93 or 696.56.58.64.

(Pastor Godson T. Nembo & Prayer Storm Team)

HOW TO USE THIS DAILY PRAYER GUIDE

I have discovered that some people do not know how to use this book well. As a result, they are not benefiting much from it. I will like to explain to you, how you can either use it during your personal prayer time or how to use it to lead a group prayer session.

Your Personal Prayer Time:

1. **Read the topic of the day:** It is the summary of the message of the day.
2. **Read the Bible passages of the day aloud:** You retain more, when you read aloud to yourself. In the early days, scriptures were read aloud.
3. **Read the meditation slowly:** Do it with a strong desire to understand.
4. **Pray the prayer points:** Read each prayer point and take time to pray well before you read the next one.
5. **Pray for others:** Use the prayer point to pray for other people as inspired by the Holy Spirit.
6. **Add other prayer topics:** For instance; dedicate your day, your family, your job, your Church, etc. to God.
7. Pray for your specific needs and those of others.
8. **Prophetic Prayers of the Week:** These prayers will be brought up every Monday. We encourage you to pray them every day during the week that follows.

Leading a Group to Pray:

1. Read the topic of the day aloud.
2. Assign one or more persons to read the Bible passage of the day aloud.

3. Read the meditation of the day aloud. After reading, you can make some comments, if necessary.
4. Allow other members of the group to make contributions or ask questions, if they have them.
5. Read one prayer point at a time. Then allow the people to pray for some time before you read the next one.
6. After they have prayed in chorus, you can ask one person to raise his/her voice and pray.
7. When you finish reading the prayer points, first ask the group members to give their own personal prayer plan.
8. At the end, let one person pray and conclude the session.

Bible Reading Plan:

We have included two Bible reading plans: **"Bible in 1 year"** and **"Bible in 2 years."** You can read through your Bible in one year by following the first plan in two years by following the second plan. Set aside time every day to read your Bible.

Thursday 1 May   **BE DILIGENT**

Read: Proverbs 6:4-11

> **Bible in 1 year:** Luke 22-24
> **Bible in 2 years:** Psa. 106

"Lazy people are soon poor; hard workers get rich"
(Proverbs 10:4 NLT).

If you want financial prosperity, you must obey God's Word, which commands us to work hard. Whatever you put in, you will reap a thirty, sixty, or a hundred-fold return. Galatians 6:7 says, *"Don't be misled—you cannot mock the justice of God. You will always harvest what you plant"* (NLT).

Proverbs 6:6-8 tells us that ants are prosperous because they are industrious and diligent. How? They mind their own business and work hard without supervision and coercion. Friend, if you sincerely want the financial prosperity you have been confessing, you must learn to work hard like ants without supervision.

Do you want to experience a supernatural financial breakthrough? It is not enough to make empty confessions about the great things you want to see in your life; you must obey God's Word. You can have what you declare, but you must take action to bring it into manifestation. Faith without works (action) is dead faith that cannot produce results. *"What good is it, dear brothers and sisters, if you say you have faith but don't show it by your actions? Can that kind of faith save anyone?"* *(James 2:14 NLT)*. Friend, if you believe God for something, begin to take action about it.

When a confession has no corresponding actions, it is a dead and useless claim. If you claim prosperity, you must courageously go out there and look for something to do. You must work hard. I read about a young man who received a prophecy from a guest preacher, announcing to him how God would prosper him abundantly that year. After service, his friend asked the man of God, "Is there a word for me from the Lord." "I have nothing to say for now," responded the guest speaker. This young man took his destiny into his own hands, worked very hard that year, and made more progress than his friend who had received the prophecy.

Put God's Word to work, and your life will never remain the same.

Let us pray

1. *Father, thank You because Your Word will not fail in my life, in Jesus' name.*
2. *Father, my destiny is settled in Christ; it shall fully manifest, in Jesus' name.*
3. *Father, every labor has profit; I receive the grace to work hard and make extraordinary progress, in Jesus' name.*
4. *Prosperity answers to hard and smart work; I receive wisdom to work intelligently, in Jesus' name.*
5. *Father, I receive grace to put Your Word to work in my life, in Jesus' name.*
6. *Father, deliver me from spiritual and mental laziness, in Jesus' name.*

Friday 2 May

SECRETS OF A
FRUITFUL LIFE 1

Read: 2 Chronicles 26:3-8

> **Bible in 1 year:** Judges 1-4
> **Bible in 2 years:** Psa. 107

"No branch can bear fruits by itself; it must remain in the vine. Neither can you bear fruit unless you remain in me…if you remain in me and I in you, you will bear much fruit; apart from me you can do nothing" (John 15:4-5).

Closeness is a secret to fruitfulness. A couple cannot bear fruit unless they become intimate—this biological law cannot be broken. Similarly, a human being cannot bear spiritual fruits without closeness to God. Your closeness with consecrated and dedicated disciples of Jesus Christ also facilitates your spiritual transformation and maturity. Show me someone who walks closely with a God-fearing believer, and I will show you a genuine disciple of Christ in the making.

Closeness with God is a vital spiritual quality you must pursue. For example, the closer you are to fire, the warmer you feel. I have observed that people who are shallow in seeking God's presence bear fewer fruits than diligent seekers. Can you be described as a diligent seeker of God? Could it be that you have become too busy to seek God?

In Mark 12:34, Jesus said to someone, *"You are not from the Kingdom."* Obviously, He was not talking about a physical distance. He was describing the man's spiritual proximity to God's Kingdom. This implies that if a man can be spiritually near the Kingdom, he can also be spiritually far from God's Kingdom. Hence, it is crucial to maintain a close spiritual connection with God.

The branch is supposed to be deeply rooted in the vine for fruits to be borne. Friend, the closer you get to God, the more you are anointed. This results in an abundance of fruits in your life. You may ask me, "How can I be close to God?" It is simple! Draw near to God, and He will draw near to you (James 4:8). Take time to go and wait on God, and you will experience the beauty of His presence and glory.

A carrier of God's presence cannot be barren!

Let us pray

1. *Father, thank You because You faithfully reveal Yourself to every sincere and diligent seeker, in Jesus' name.*
2. *Father, today, I sacrifice anything trying to take me away from Your presence on the altar, in Jesus' name.*
3. *Father, fill me with Your Spirit and stir an unquenchable hunger for Your presence in me, in Jesus' name.*
4. *Fire of God, fall on me now and consume every veil of spiritual blindness responsible for shallow Christianity, in Jesus' name.*
5. *Father, fill me with wisdom to follow those following You sincerely, in Jesus' name.*
6. *Father, some people are seeking the truth who need guidance; send me to them, in Jesus' name.*

**SECRETS OF A
FRUITFUL LIFE 2**

Read: Hebrews 12:3-13

> **Bible in 1 year:** Judges 5-8
> **Bible in 2 years:** Psa. 108-109

"He cuts off every branch in me that bears no fruit, while every branch that does bear fruit, he prunes, so that it will be more fruitful" (John 15:2).

God will cut off every barren branch but purge you because you bear fruit. Why? So that you can bear abundant fruit. To prune or Purge is a semi-aggressive process of removing unwanted qualities. When God is purging you, it means He puts you in a challenging condition to force you to expel, eject, clear out, dismiss, discharge, eradicate, or exclude something negative from your life.

Many painful events in our lives are purging processes. Suffering through crises and troubles often clears unwanted attitudes and qualities from our lives. I have witnessed dramatic transformations in the lives of some believers after they have experienced a fiery trial. It is like some attitudes in our lives can only be dealt with by fire. A problematic marriage can purge you of unwanted pride. The loss of a job may purge you of your arrogance. The loss of money may purge you of foolishness. It is impossible to describe the purging process God has ordained for you. However, expect to be purged by the Lord as long as you are bearing fruits in the Lord Jesus Christ.

The purging process is quite unpleasant, but the results have an eternal impact on your destiny (vs. 11). Instead of getting discouraged because of your difficulty, focus on the harvest of righteousness and peace that is coming. God cannot allow you to face a situation you cannot bear (1 Corinthians 10:13). If He has permitted it, then you can handle it. Turn to Him for grace and wisdom to guide you through it.

Every trial has an expiry date. Do not ruin the process by becoming bitter. Remember, you will go through the same cycle if you fail your test. Receive the grace to triumph, in Jesus' name.

Let us pray

1. *Father, thank You because Your plan for me is life of abundant fruitfulness.*
2. *Father, for profound work of transformation ongoing in my life, in Jesus' name.*
3. *O Lord, I surrender to Your pruning process; perfect Your work in my life, in Jesus' name.*
4. *Father, you are more interested in my transformation than my comfort; help me to submit wholly to Your will for my life, in Jesus' name.*
5. *Father, people's opinion is not Your will; help to stick to Your will and plan for my life, in Jesus' name.*
6. *Father, strengthen Your children reading this message who are facing trials, to abide in Your will with joy, in Jesus' name.*

Sunday 4 May   **SECRETS OF A**
                                    FRUITFUL LIFE 3

Read: Isaiah 32:13-15

> **Bible in 1 year:** Judges 9-12
> **Bible in 2 years:** Psa. 110-111

"Till the Spirit is poured on us from on high, and the desert becomes a fruitful field, and the fertile field seems like a forest" (Isaiah 32:15).

The presence of the Holy Spirit in your life will make you abundantly fruitful. The absence of the work of the Holy Spirit causes dryness and fruitlessness in your life. Wherever the Holy Spirit is at work, there is visible transformation and fruitfulness. Friend, things will change when the Holy Spirit is poured on you. You will become fruitful. When you become anointed, you become fruitful – full of fruits and results.

The Holy Spirit made Jesus Christ fruitful. Luke 4:18 says about Him, *"The Spirit of the Lord is upon me because He has anointed me to preach the gospel to the poor; He has sent me to heal the brokenhearted, to preach deliverance to the captives, and recovering of sight to the blind, to set at liberty those that are bruised..."* The Holy Spirit was the secret behind Jesus' fruitful ministry. Is your ministry barren, without tangible results to show for your labor? The Holy Spirit will come on you and terminate the barrenness. Before Jesus received the Holy Spirit, He was an obscure carpenter in Nazareth. After the experience, His fame spread like wildfire. Your story will change.

The Holy Spirit made Jesus' Disciples fruitful. After they received the power of the Holy Spirit on the day of Pentecost, signs and wonders became common among them. As a result, several people were saved and added to the Kingdom. The silent and confused disciples exploded with power, shaking their generation for the Lord.

The Holy Spirit is God's strategy for terminating every form of barrenness in your life. Our key verse says, "Till the Spirit is poured on us from on high…" The Word "Till" or "Until" means a time of waiting or a period of preparation before a significant event. You have to seek God passionately and patiently for the pouring of the Holy Spirit in your life. Speaking in tongues is not enough; seek God's power.

Let us pray

1. *Father, thank You because You will send the Holy Spirit to terminate barrenness in my life, in Jesus' name.*
2. *Present that area of barrenness to the Lord and pray for healing and restoration, in Jesus' name.*
3. *Father, give me the grace to seek You till Your glory saturates my life, in Jesus' name.*
4. *Father, rent the heavens over us and pour Your Spirit mightily upon us, in Jesus' name.*
5. *Father, arise in my life and turn my barren ministry into a fruitful field, in Jesus' name.*
6. *Father, send us the rain of revival for renewal and restoration in Your work, in Jesus' name.*

Monday 5 May **ENJOYING**
ABUNDANT LIFE

Read: Ephesians 3:14-21

Bible in 1 year: Judges 13-15
Bible in 2 years: Psa. 112-113

"The thief comes only to steal and kill and destroy; I have come that they may have life, and have it to the full" (John 10:10).

There is a quality of life we have been called to live in Christ. It is called abundant life. Are you enjoying it? In John 10:10, Jesus said, *"The thief does not come except to steal, and to kill, and to destroy. I have come that they may have life, and that they may it more abundantly."* What does the "Abundant life" we are talking about look like? First, look at these words: "Life" and "Abundantly." "Life" comes from the Greek word *'Zoe'*, which means "The absolute fullness of life." "Abundantly" used in this biblical account is the Greek word *'Perissos,'* which means "Over and above, more than is necessary, superadded." Simply put, God wants us to enjoy eternal life (Supernatural life) over and above, more than necessary, and exceeding normal measures.

But the problem is that most believers ignorantly relegate eternal life to some future experience when, in fact, we are called to enjoy a supernatural life here and now. You don't have to wait until you die to experience eternal life. God doesn't want us to barely survive while waiting for heaven. He wants us to enjoy the abundant life which is a life of victory.

28

The question is, how do we enjoy this abundant life? Paul wrote in his Epistle to the Ephesians, *"Now unto him that is able to do exceeding abundantly above all that we ask or think, according to the power that worketh in us" (vs. 20 KJV)*. The phrase "Exceeding abundantly" is the same term Jesus used to describe the life He came to give us. In other words, God desires us to live above circumstances, pain, fear, sickness, rejection, and any other limitations presented to us in the natural realm. He wants us to experience an overcoming life – a life of true victory. The key is found in this phrase, *"According to the power that works in us."* If you want to enjoy the abundant life, you must place a demand on it by faith according to the power of the Spirit that is working in you. The greater the demand, the greater the supply!

Let us pray

1. *Father, thank You for giving abundant and eternal life in Christ.*
2. *Father, thank You for Your abundant life at work in me, in Jesus' name.*
3. *Father, help me always see myself from Your perspective, not the way the world sees, in Jesus' name.*
4. *Healing and restoration are flowing in me because of the presence of God's life in me, in Jesus' name.*
5. *My life is moving from glory to glory and strength to strength because of God's life at work in me, in Jesus' name.*
6. *I will not fail or fall because God's life sustains me, in Jesus' name.*

Prophetic Prayers of the Week

1. *The Holy Spirit is at work in me; I will bear abundant fruits of a godly character, in Jesus' name.*

2. *The blessing of the LORD is upon me; the works of my hands will prosper, increase, and multiply abundantly this month, in Jesus' name.*

3. *The enemies of my destiny will not succeed against me this month, in Jesus' name.*

SPEAK TO THE
                                    SITUATION

Read: Jeremiah 1:4-8; Numbers 14:26-31

> **Bible in 1 year:** Judges 16-18
> **Bible in 2 years:** Psa. 114-115

"So, tell them, 'As surely as I live,' declares the LORD, 'I will do the very things I hear you say" (Numbers 14:28 NIV).

God has given you power on your tongue to command change in your life. If you don't like what is going on in your life, you can change it by what you say. You can alter your future by what you say today.

If you want to know where you will be in five years, listen to your words. Whether you realize it or not, any time you speak, you are prophesying your future. If you want to be stronger, healthier, and happier in the days ahead, start to declare it now.

We talk more to ourselves than we do to anybody else. The question is what are you saying to yourself? Jeremiah was still young and inexperienced when he heard God's promises. Rather than feeling blessed, he was afraid and said, "God, I can't do that. I can't speak to nations. I am too young. I wouldn't even know what to say." But God answered, "Jeremiah, say not that you are young." There are things you should not say about yourself because they will destroy your destiny.

Negative words hinder God's promises from materializing in our lives. It is wrong to limit God through the negative confessions of your lips. Never forget that God responds to us according to what we speak into His ears. Never be deceived into thinking that you can talk anyhow and still live well.

All the Israelites who chose to complain and murmur against God died in the wilderness of various plagues because they declared so over their lives. What are you saying concerning your life?

From today, stop cursing your destiny with negative words and start blessing yourself. You will be satisfied with good things through the fruit of your lips. Have you not read in the Bible that when you decree things, they come to pass (Job 22:28)? Start declaring today, "It shall be well with me, and I will eat the fruit of my doing, in Jesus' name" (Isaiah 3:10).

Let us pray

1. *Father, anoint my ears to hear Your voice clearer this month, in Jesus' name.*
2. *Father, may I not miss my Word for breakthrough this month, in Jesus' name.*
3. *Father, I loose my soul from the captivity of murmuring and complaining, in Jesus' name.*
4. *I begin to root out every destructive word others and I have declared over my destiny, in Jesus' name.*
5. *Merciful Father, arise and begin to restore every area of my life that negative words have destroyed, in Jesus' name.*
6. *Begin to decree the good things you want to see in your life right now, in Jesus' name.*

THE SACRIFICE OF A HERO

Read: Genesis 22:1-10

> **Bible in 1 year:** Judges 19-21
> **Bible in 2 years:** Psa. 116-117

"It is by faith Abraham offered Isaac as a sacrifice when God was testing him. Abraham who had received God's promises, was ready to sacrifice his only son, Isaac" (Hebrews 11:17 NLT).

One mark of a hero is the capacity to make outstanding sacrifices. True heroes are not famous because of titles they claim but because of their uncommon exploits. Abraham is a hero of faith because of the quality of sacrifices he made for God.

At age 99, Abraham entered into a covenant with God. A year later, Isaac was born. This marked the beginning of the generations of Abraham and his seed after him. God demanded the sacrifice of his dear son Isaac, whom he loved dearly. Abraham understood the implication of sacrificing his only son, who represented the seed God had promised him. Isaac was the future of his family. Losing him meant losing everything. Yet, he refused to yield to human logic. He had decided to follow God, and he was not backing off. He had made some mistakes before, but he would not repeat the same mistakes this time.

Abraham went to the mountain early the following day to honor his covenant with God. This was proof of his love and loyalty to God. Today, many sing, "Abraham's blessings are mine..." They want Abraham's blessings but are unwilling to make the same type of sacrifice that Abraham did.

The secret of greatness is tied to outstanding sacrifices. This is what will make you a hero. Do you desire to be great in God's Kingdom? Don't shy away from sacrifices. Demonstrate your love for God by your heartfelt sacrifices.

Let us pray

1. *Father, thank You for the sacrifice of Jesus Christ on the cross that has given me access into God's eternal family, in Jesus' name.*
2. *Father, thank You because every sacrifice I make for the Gospel's sake brings blessings and increase, in Jesus' name.*
3. *Father, fill my heart with fresh fire to live a life of sacrifice, in Jesus' name.*
4. *O Father, teach me how to sacrifice things that matter to me for Your glory, in Jesus' name.*
5. *Father, I submit to Your will; as the cross of Jesus Christ deals with the flesh, let me increase in Your power, wisdom, and understanding, in Jesus' name.*
6. *Father, use me to do extraordinary things for Your glory, in Jesus' name.*

34

Thursday 8 May   **SAVE IN YOUR**
                                      ETERNAL HOME

Read: Matthew 6:19-21

> **Bible in 1 year:** Ruth 1-4
> **Bible in 2 years:** Psa. 118

"Though I appreciate your gifts, what makes me happiest is the well-earned reward you will have because of your kindness" (Philippians 4:17 TLB).

Yaou invest in your eternal home any time you are generous. Jesus called this principle "Storing up treasure in heaven." He used this phrase six times in the Bible! You should not take anything Jesus talks about six times lightly. If you do, you are certainly going to miss a blessing.

In our reading, Jesus says, *"Don't store up treasures here on earth, where moths eat them and rust destroys them, and where thieves break in and steal. Store your treasures in heaven, where moths and rust cannot destroy, and thieves do not break in and steal" (Matthew 6:19-20 NLT)*. Friend, giving is saving in your heavenly account.

Most people live less than 100 years on this planet, after which they must leave all their earthly treasures behind and go to heaven or hell. But God's will for you is that you will get to enjoy your heavenly treasure for eternity.

So, how do you store up treasure in heaven? How do you send it ahead before you leave this world? You do it by investing in God's work and people. God wants you to invest in people because those investments have eternal consequences and rewards. Only two things will last forever: (1) God's Word and (2) People. People will spend eternity in either heaven or hell, and your investment in someone could make all the difference.

In our main verse, Paul says, *"Though I appreciate your gifts, what makes me happiest is the well-earned reward you will have because of your kindness" (Philippians 4:17 TLB).*
He wrote to the Philippians to express his appreciation for their support. But he said what was more important was knowing that their sacrifice and generosity gave them treasure in heaven. They invested in their eternal home by investing in Paul.

Invest in your eternal home by sacrificing your time, money, and material things for the good of others. You will not miss your reward.

Let us pray

1. *Father, thank You for blessing me to become a blessing for others, in Jesus' name.*
2. *Father, may I never miss any opportunity You give me to save in my heavenly account, in Jesus' name.*
3. *There are needs in some people's lives I must meet this season; guide me to them, in Jesus' name.*
4. *Father, deliver me from the receiving mentality and give me a giving mentality, in Jesus' name.*
5. *Father, let Your grace cause generosity to manifest in all the domains of my life, in Jesus' name.*
6. *Father, teach me how to make profit in all my work this year, in Jesus' name.*

GOD TESTS YOU WITH MONEY

Read: Luke 16:10-13

> **Bible in 1 year:** 1Pet. 1-2
> **Bible in 2 years:** Psa. 119:1-32

"Don't store up treasures here on earth, where moths eat them and rust destroys them, and where thieves break in and steal. Store your treasures in heaven, where moths and rust cannot destroy, and thieves do not break in and steal. Wherever your treasure is, there the desires of your heart will also be" (Matthew 6:19-21 NLT).

One way God tests you is with money. If He can trust you with material possessions, then He can trust you with true riches in heaven.

God uses money to test different areas of your life. Take note of these:

1. *Money shows what you love most:* If you really want to know what's important to you, look at how you spend your time and money. They clearly show what you love most. Matthew 6:19-21 says, *'Don't store up treasures here on earth . . . Store your treasures in heaven . . . Wherever your treasure is, there the desires of your heart will also be" (NLT).* Put your money wherever you want your heart to be. Do you know that you will become interested in whatever you invest in? **If you love God, you will give Him your money.**

2. **Money shows what you trust most:** Money is the acid test for faith. The Bible says, *"Those who trust in their riches will fall, but the righteous will thrive like a green leaf" (Proverbs 11:28 NIV)*. Do you trust in your money for security, or do you trust in God? Do you trust in your money to make you happy, or do you trust in God for your happiness? The way you use money will reveal whom you trust.

3. **Money shows if God can trust you:** How you use money shows if God can trust you. Luke 16:10-12 says, *"If you are faithful in little things, you will be faithful in large ones. But if you are dishonest in little things, you won't be honest with greater responsibilities. And if you are untrustworthy about worldly wealth, who will trust you with the true riches of heaven? And if you are not faithful with other people's things, why should you be trusted with things of your own?" (NLT)*.

How you handle money affects how much God blesses you and commits Kingdom resources into your hands. Now that you understand that managing money well attracts God's blessing, ask Him to help you put your finances in order so that He can trust you with true riches.

Let us pray
1. *Father, thank You for blessing me with the means to serve You.*
2. *Father, deliver my soul from the love of money, in Jesus' name.*
3. *Father, in any way I have failed the money test, please forgive and restore me, in Jesus' name.*
4. *Father, rule my heart and teach me how to invest in the Kingdom, in Jesus' name.*

5. *Father, the fear of losing money is the beginning of stinginess; teach me how to use money, in Jesus' name.*
6. *Givers never lack; may I not miss any opportunity to give this month, in Jesus' name.*

Saturday 10 May   **CHANGE THE WAY**
                                        YOU THINK

Read: Proverbs 4:20-24

> **Bible in 1 year:** 1Pet. 3-6
> **Bible in 2 years:** Psa. 119:33-64

"Be careful how you think; your life is shaped by your thoughts" (Proverbs 4:23 GNT).

To change your circumstances, change the way you think!
God is far more interested in changing your mind than changing your circumstances.

I know you want God to remove all your problems, pain, sorrow, suffering, sickness, and sadness. But He wants to work on you first because change will not happen until you renew your mind (Romans 12:1-2). So, why is it crucial for you to learn how to control your mind? Here are three reasons:

1. ***Your thoughts control your life:*** Proverbs 4:23 says, *"Be careful how you think; your life is shaped by your thoughts" (GNT).* Your thoughts have a tremendous ability to shape your life for good or for evil. For example, maybe you have accepted the insult or the evil voice in your dreams that tells you, "You are worthless. You will never amount to anything good." If you have accepted that thought as truth, it will negatively shape your life. What are the negative thoughts that are controlling your mind?

40

2. **Your mind is the battleground for sin:** Paul says in Romans 7:22-23, *"I love to do God's will so far as my new nature is concerned; but there is something else deep within me, in my lower nature, that is at war with my mind and wins the fight and makes me a slave to the sin that is still within me. In my mind I want to be God's willing servant, but instead I find myself still enslaved to sin" (TLB).* Sometimes, you get mentally fatigued because of the battles going on in your brain 24/7. The battles are severe because your mind is your greatest asset, and Satan wants to control it.

3. **Your mind is the key to your peace and happiness:** A mind that the enemy controls leads to tension, stress, and conflicts. Meanwhile, you enjoy tranquility and confidence when you rule your mind with God's Word. Friend, do you want to enjoy strength, security, and serenity? Take charge of your mind and direct it with God's Word.

Let us pray
1. *Father, thank You for giving me the mind of Christ, in Jesus' name.*
2. *Father, let Your light shine in me and expose every evil thought that Satan is trying to use against me, in Jesus' name.*
3. *Blood of Jesus Christ, begin to purify my mind of every pollution by negative thoughts, in Jesus' name.*
4. *Place your hand on your forehead and pray 5 times, "Fire of God, burn now and consume every unclean thought in me, in Jesus' name."*
5. *I root out every thought of... (mention the name) from my mind, in Jesus' name.*

6. *Begin to plant healthy and godly thoughts in your mind (peace, love, joy, etc.).*

Read: Matthew 16:13-20

> **Bible in 1 year:** 2Pet. 1-3
> **Bible in 2 years:** Psa. 119:65-88

"Who do men say that I, the Son of Man, am?"
(Matthew 16:13).

What people say about you can help you evaluate and refocus your life. That is why you should not be upset when people confront you with issues about your life. In our text, Jesus asked His Disciples to critique His ministry. Through it, His identity was revealed to His disciples more deeply.

Every time we open our eyes, light enters our pupils and shines into our retina. Inside the retina are photoreceptors—nerve cells that transmit information to the brain. That is how we see things. However, there is a small area of our retina without photoreceptors. This is described as our blind spot. Consequently, we cannot interpret the light shown in that section.

In life, blind spots are things others quickly see in us, but we don't see in ourselves. They are aspects of ourselves that we are usually unaware of. We can call them our weaknesses.

How can you discover your blind spot? Like Jesus Christ, you can do it by asking some of your intimate and trusted friends to provide honest feedback on your appearance, character, work ethic, relationships, table

43

manners, personal hygiene, financial matters, study habits, attitude towards customers/clients, and your approach to tasks. If these people genuinely love you and you are open to them, they will point out things that will improve your life if you adjust to them.

Knowing your blind spot can help you gain perspective on adjusting your behavior and guard against your weaknesses. However, this can only work when you take action to change. Be intentional about character transformation.

Everyone has a blind spot. Identifying and dealing with it makes you a better person.

Let us pray

1. *Father, thank You because nothing concerning me is hidden before You, in Jesus' name.*
2. *Father, shine Your light and expose my blind spots to me and my friends, in Jesus' name.*
3. *Father, give me the grace to accept constructive criticism so that I can grow, in Jesus' name.*
4. *Father, surround me with people who can help me grow, in Jesus' name.*
5. *Father, please help me not to miss any season You have ordained for me this year, in Jesus' name.*
6. *Father, help me to master any bad habit in me Satan wants to use to ruin my destiny, in Jesus' name.*

Monday 12 May   **BOUNCE BACK**

Read: Micah 7:7-10; Prov. 24:16-17

> **Bible in 1 year:** 1Thess. 4-5
> **Bible in 2 years:** Psa. 119:89-120

"Do not rejoice over me, my enemy; when I fall, I will arise…" (Micah 7:8).

No failure is final in life. This implies that wherever you have fallen, you can arise and do greater exploits with God. Prophet Micah believed this: *"Do not rejoice over me, my enemy, when I fall, I will arise."* Friend, God's hand is released today to bring you out of every pit, in Jesus' name.

Sadly, some people have a superhuman approach to life. They cannot imagine themselves making mistakes. They see others who have made mistakes as failures. This perfectionist tendency has crippled such people to the point of nonperformance or inertia. On the other hand, some who refuse to give up achieve remarkable breakthroughs after several attempts.

As human beings, we are prone to making mistakes. That is why we should avoid expecting perfection from our children, spouses, friends, and family members. In July 2024, I met a lovely man in the gym in Los Angeles, USA, and we had a wonderful time exercising every morning. In early January 2025, I received a sad message: "Jerry is dead. He committed suicide." When I asked why, I was told that he got discouraged because of his children's poor performance in school. How many have destroyed themselves because they couldn't deal with failure?

Your failure is not the end. The mistake you made has not sealed your destiny. God wants to turn things around for you. Make up your mind not to give up. A story is told of a player who mistakenly scored a goal against his team. At halftime, his team was down by one goal. Everyone was uncomfortable with the costly mistake and thought the coach would replace the player. Surprisingly, the coach hugged him, said, "I understand you," and didn't replace him. This player was poised to do better and scored the equalizing and winning goals.

You are not a failure because you failed. Bounce back in Jesus' name!

Let us pray

1. *Father, thank You because my fall has not made me a failure; I can bounce back, in Jesus' name.*
2. *Father, I make up my mind today to bounce back from where I have fallen; help me, in Jesus' name.*
3. *Father, release into my life anything I need to bounce back where I have fallen, in Jesus' name.*
4. *Father, my name is not a failure; where I am now is not my destination; I am moving forward, in Jesus' name.*
5. *Place your hand on your chest and pray 5 times, "I receive new fire for my next level, in Jesus' name."*
6. *Father, with You, nothing is lost. Begin to pray for restoration in your own life and in the lives of others.*

Prophetic Prayers of the Week

1. *I am the apple of God's eye; no evil hand will prevail over me this week, in Jesus' name.*

2. *The God of truth, justice, and peace will fight for me, and I will hold my peace, in Jesus' name.*

3. *Whatever evil programmed against my family and I by ancestral spirits is aborted, in Jesus' name.*

Tuesday 13 May   **DON'T TREAT SIN LIGHTLY**

Read: Proverbs 28:13-14

> **Bible in 1 year:** Psa. 1-3
> **Bible in 2 years:** Psa. 119:121-144

"He was manifested to take away our sins" (1 John 3:5).

Our Bible reading reveals the two ways people deal with sin: they confess and abandon it or conceal and ignore it, then go on with life as if nothing serious had happened.

You have to know that when you refuse to confront your sins and deal with them correctly, you expose your life and that of your family to satanic attacks. A good biblical example is King David, who committed adultery with the wife of one of his military commanders, Uriah. Instead of repenting of his adultery, he went on and murdered Uriah because he wanted to conceal his sin. His poor handling of the sin provoked terrible curses on his family (1 Samuel 11-12). The way some people deal with sin seems like they think that when you successfully conceal a sinful act from public view, it is buried forever. No! The Bible clearly states, *"Whoever conceals his transgressions will not prosper, but he who confesses and forsakes them will obtain mercy" (Proverbs 28:13).*

Concerning those who laugh at others who have fallen into sin and boastfully say, "I can never do that," without building strong spiritual walls around their lives, the Bible says, *"If you think you are standing strong, be careful not to fall" (1 Corinthians 10:12 NLT).* If you fail to deal with sin appropriately, you may find yourself doing the things you had vowed never to do. Considering David's fervent zeal in serving God, one would never have imagined that he could commit adultery and murder.

Another danger of failing to deal with your sin correctly is that God can give up on you. About this, Paul wrote, *"As they did not think it worthwhile to retain the knowledge of God…[he] gave them over to a depraved mind, so that they do what ought not to be done" (Romans 1:28 NIV)*. This is the worst that can happen to you; that God gives you over to your carnal desires and says, "Do what you like."

But the good news today is that *"He was manifested to take away our sins" (1 John 3:5)*. You can be free from sin if you are ready to repent, restitute, and allow the Holy Spirit to deal with your character.

Let us pray
1. *Holy Father, thank You for sending Jesus Christ to remove my sins.*
2. *Are there certain issues you have to deal with before God? Take time and deal with them now.*
3. *Are there some issues you have to deal with someone? Decide what you have to do within the next one week.*
4. *Fire of God, burn the root of…(name the sin) in my heart and set me free, in the name of Jesus.*
5. *Father, give me grace to put to death the works of the flesh in my life, in the name of Jesus.*
6. *Holy Spirit, fill our hearts and cause the righteousness of God to flourish among us, in the name of Jesus.*

Wednesday 14 May   **WAIT IN PRAYER AND FASTING**

Read: Luke 2:36-38

> **Bible in 1 year:** Psa. 4-6
> **Bible in 2 years:** Psa. 119:145-176

"Then she lived as a widow to the age of eighty-four. She never left the Temple but stayed there day and night, worshiping God with fasting and prayer" (Luke 2:37 NLT).

Prayer is the force that moves God's hand to change the world. Until we wait in prayer, we may not enjoy certain victories.

The story of Anna in our text inspires us to practice the art of waiting on God. After her husband's death at a young age, she waited in prayer and fasting in the temple until she was eighty-four years old. The Bible says, *"She never left the Temple but stayed there day and night, worshipping God with fasting and prayer" (vs. 37).* Miraculously, God kept her alive until she saw the consolation of Israel at the advent of Jesus Christ.

Today, many people have a thousand and one reasons why they can't find time to fast and pray. Recently, I gave out some write-ups in a group, including prayer topics on "How to pray for your husband, your wife, your children, and your career." Somebody sent me a WhatsApp message: "Good evening, pastor. I have a worry. I don't know how to organize myself to pray. I work during the day, and I have an eight-month-old baby." To this person, prayer is a heavy task that cannot be added to the load of responsibilities she is carrying.

Friend, are you in a situation where you think you are too busy to pray? The truth is, if you are too busy to find time and fellowship with your Creator in prayer, be sure that you will soon become a prey to the enemy. A day without prayer leaves a believer weak. Great saints of old were people of prayer. They routed the kingdoms of darkness with the power of prayer. Esther fasted for three days without food and water, and became an instrument of deliverance for Israel.

Fasting is not outdated. Mighty power is generated through it. When did you last wait on the LORD in prayer and fasting? Yield to the Holy Spirit and wait on God!

Let us pray

1. *Father, thank You for Your mighty power generated through prayer and fasting, in Jesus' name.*
2. *Father, deliver my soul from the laziness to fast and pray, in Jesus' name.*
3. *Father, give me the grace to root out of my life the things that are killing my prayer life, in Jesus' name.*
4. *Father, pour Your Spirit afresh on us and restore the passion to pray mightily, in Jesus' name.*
5. *I bind and cast out every anti-prayer spirit fighting me, my family, and Church, in Jesus' name.*
6. *Present any present need you have to God. He will answer you.*

Thursday 15 May   **DON'T FAINT**

Read: 2 Corinthians 4:8-18

> **Bible in 1 year:** Psa. 7-9
> **Bible in 2 years:** Psa. 120-122

"For which cause we faint not; but though our outward man perish, yet the inward man is renewed day by day" (2 Corinthians 4:16).

Y ou need an unbreakable faith to fulfill your destiny in Christ. Why? Sometimes, God's mission for us is so tough that we will give up and quit if we lack rugged faith. What made Apostle Paul say, *"For which cause we faint not!" (2 Corinthians 4:16)*? It was faith. He fully trusted in the Lord Jesus Christ to carry him through.

In thirty-seven years, Missionary William Milne (1785-1822) made a dramatic impact on God's work through his radical consecration and dedication to God. After his conversion as a teenager, Milne volunteered to join the London Missionary Society and became their missionary to China. He undertook the arduous task of learning a new language with a willing spirit. He once said, "Learning the Chinese language requires bodies of iron, lungs of brass, heads of oak, hands of spring steel, eyes of eagles, hearts of apostles, memories of angels, and lives of Methuselah." Yet, despite the hardship, he persisted and became an expert in the Chinese language.

Minle buried his wife and two infant children in the mission field before dying himself at 37. During his time in

China, he helped found churches and a Bible college and wrote and edited two missionary magazines. Hundreds were saved as a result of his efforts. His refusal to yield to difficulty made his ministry a lasting success. Two of his children followed him into full-time ministry, and his testimony encouraged many to follow him to the mission field.

All of us face difficulties in our Christian journey. However, faith is the difference between those who give up and those who accomplish great exploits with God. Those who succeed have strong faith enough to trust God through harsh trials and continue investing in His work. This is the faith we need today to impact our world. Apostle Paul demonstrated it. It is a never-giving-up spirit. Ask God for it!

Let us pray

1. *Father, thank You because in Christ I am unbreakable.*
2. *Father, thank You because I can do the things You have assigned for me, in Jesus' name.*
3. *Father, fill me with the strength I need to accomplish my Kingdom assignment, in Jesus' name.*
4. *Father, expand my capacity to carry the burden of the ministry You have assigned to me, in Jesus' name.*
5. *Father, deliver my soul from procrastination and laziness in Jesus' name.*
6. *Father, teach me to rely on Your power to do Your work, not on my strength, in Jesus' name.*

Read: Joshua 3:1-6

> **Bible in 1 year:** Psa. 10-12
> **Bible in 2 years:** Psa. 123-125

"And Joshua said to the people, 'Sanctify yourselves, for tomorrow the LORD will do wonders among you'" *(Joshua 3:5).*

After forty years of wandering in the wilderness, the children of Israel were now getting set to go out and possess the land of Canaan. They needed to receive precise instructions to walk in God's will. They also needed divine covering as they engaged the occupants of the Promised Land in fierce battles. They were to sanctify and present themselves as living sacrifices to God to guarantee divine backing. Considering the great things God has reserved for us this year, we must continuously carry out thorough spiritual checks and indeed amend our ways so that we may live under divine covering every day.

1. ***Check your spiritual foundation:*** What is the root, source, and strength of your life? Is it Jesus Christ or something else? (Ephesians 2:20). Let Jesus become all you count on.

2. ***Check your heart:*** What are your thoughts centered on? How pure is your heart? What do you meditate on all day long? Are you preoccupied with the things of

54

eternal value or overwhelmed by the selfish ambition and pleasures of this world? Let your heart be fully dedicated to Jesus Christ.

3. ***Check your lifestyle:*** Do the things you do contribute to fulfilling your divine destiny? Is your lifestyle a shining light that serves as a witness among the unsaved? Begin to do everything as unto Jesus Christ (Colossians 3: 23).

4. ***Check your priority:*** Who occupies the first place in your life? Is it God or other things? One secret to excelling this year is setting God's kingdom and righteousness on your agenda.

5. ***Check your focus:*** What is your focus? Is it on earthly things or heavenly things? Refocus your life and become a heavenly-minded Christian. Refuse to gain the world and lose your soul in hell.

6. ***Check your relationships:*** Who are your closest friends? Are you walking with the wise so that you can become wise? Are you walking with those who fear and love God so that you can grow in the faith? It is time to cut off from fools so that you will not be destroyed by them.

It is time to check yourself and be sure you are fit for divine purpose. Don't tolerate anything that can hinder the manifestation of God's glory.

Let us pray

1. *Give thanks to God for every new thing He has planned to do in your life this year.*

2. *Bring your heart before God and ask the Holy Spirit to shine on your soul and spirit. Ask Him to show you the areas that need change.*

3. *Tell God I am ready to change and to walk fully in your ways. Father, take over my heart and help me.*

4. *Kneel before the Lord and consecrate your life to Him. Bring all the areas of your life to Him and commit yourself to walk in His ways.*

5. *Father, let justice, purity, and devotedness become my trademark from today, in Jesus' name.*

6. *Father, teach me how to use all you will put in my hands this year. Also, cause my light to shine brighter.*

Saturday 17 May   **PEOPLE OF**
                                       INTEGRITY
                                       NEEDED

Read: John 1:43-51; Genesis 25:29-34

> **Bible in 1 year:** Psa. 13-15
> **Bible in 2 years:** Psa. 126-128

"Jesus saw Nathaniel coming toward Him and said of him, 'Behold an Israelite indeed in whom there is no deceit" (John 1:47).

What testimony would Jesus Christ give concerning you, about money, morality, and ministry? Can He say about you, "Behold a man or woman of integrity?"

What is "Integrity?" Integrity is moral strength and firmness. It is incorruptibility, completeness, or honesty. Our God is a God of integrity who wants us to be like Him. Sadly, the world is suffering from Acute Integrity Deficiency Syndrome (AIDS). Daily, people are searching for people of integrity to work with. Businesses, marriages, and society at large are crumbling because of the deficiency of integrity. The major crisis of this generation is that we have heavy weight politicians without integrity, students and lecturers without integrity, and sadly ministers of the Gospel without integrity.

God and the world are looking for men and women of integrity: pastors with strong moral fibers who are not manipulated by either gold or vain glory; public leaders who don't soil their reputation because of a privileged position in the government; people who are faithful in the jobs entrusted to their hands; men who have been tested with women, finance, and fame and have not become a disgrace. A man dropped his purse containing a huge amount in the shop of one of our church members. He returned a few days later and the brother gave him the purse without opening it. The man was shocked and said, "This man, you will never become rich." In other words, if I were you, I would have kept the money and said, I have never seen the purse.

Are you a person of integrity like Nathaniel? Can you refuse to be identified with Esau who sold his birthright because of his immediate need? Decide today to start building a profile of integrity. It can be the key to the glorious future you dream about.

Let us pray

1. *Father, thank You because You deal with me with perfect integrity.*
2. *Examine your life. Are there areas of dishonesty and double standards? Present them to God and seek His forgiveness.*
3. *Father, walking in integrity is possible; give me the grace to do so, in Jesus' name.*
4. *Father, it requires discipline to walk in integrity; I receive the grace to live a disciplined life, in Jesus' name.*
5. *Father, You promote and work with people of integrity; please give me the heart of integrity, in Jesus' name.*
6. *Father, deliver my soul from the spirit of Esau and make me live like Nathaniel, in Jesus' name.*

Read: James 2:14-18

> **Bible in 1 year:** Psa. 16-18
> **Bible in 2 years:** Psa. 129-131

"I was known for helping people in trouble and standing up for those who were down..." (Job 29:12).

Y ou become great in God by making other people great. Jesus Christ has earned the most significant name in human history because He gave His precious life for His followers to make them great. He has set an example we should follow (1 Peter 2: 21).

Mother Theresa said, "The biggest disease today isn't leprosy or cancer. It is the feeling of being uncared for, unwanted – of being deserted and alone." Having caught this vision, she spent her life rescuing sick and abandoned babies in Calcutta, India. Asked why she did it, she replied, "Because Jesus did it." We can show compassion to the underprivileged who are littered everywhere around us because Jesus did it.

Think about this: Of the 1,189 chapters in the Bible, 250 contain the words of the prophets. That is roughly 21 percent of the whole Bible. Half of what the prophets say denounces sin, and the other half condemns those who see human suffering and do nothing about it. Today, the same events that horrified the prophets in those days are common around us, yet we seem to have become immune to human suffering.

It is dangerous to become desensitized to sin and human suffering. God expects our faith to be accompanied by works. He makes it clear: "That faith without works [of compassion] is dead" (James 2: 20). Those who live only for themselves are very small in the eyes of God, no matter how rich they are before men.

Let us pray

1. *Merciful Father, thank you because Your love, mercy, and grace have kept me alive.*
2. *O Lord, clothe me with a garment of mercy and use me this year to touch many who need Your love, in the name of Jesus.*
3. *Father, I am tired of struggling alone. Please connect me to my ministry and destiny helpers, in Jesus' name.*
4. *Father, move the hearts of church leaders in this nation to pay special attention to the plight of the poor and needy, in Jesus' name.*
5. *Pray that God will call committed workers to minister to street children in this nation.*
6. *Pray that God will call and anoint men and women to minister to drug addicts and those who are mentally sick in this nation.*

**THE VOICE OF GOD
                                            RESTORED**

Read: Genesis 3:8-13

> **Bible in 1 year:** Psa. 19-21
> **Bible in 2 years:** Psa. 132-134

"I was in the Spirit on the Lord's Day, and I heard behind me a loud voice, as of a trumpet" (Revelation 1:10).

The first thing God does to the one He wants to restore is the revelation of His voice. This is because the voice of God guarantees the knowledge of His will and His ways in your life. David prayed, *"Teach me Your way, O LORD; I will walk in Your truth" (Psalm 86:11).* This is why the manifestation of the voice of God in your life is indispensable for the fulfillment of your destiny. Prophet Isaiah said, *"Your ears shall hear a word behind you, saying, 'This is the way, walk in it,' Whenever you turn to the right hand Or whenever you turn to the left" (Isaiah 30: 21).* The question is: "Do you hear the voice of God?"

The first tragedy of the fall of man in Eden was the loss of God's voice. Adam and Eve hid themselves in the bushes when they heard the voice of God because of a guilty conscience (Genesis 3: 8). That was the beginning of mankind's alienation from God, the source of life and truth. Today, many human beings cannot identify the voice of their creator. They turn to idols, demons, and strange spirits to seek solutions for their problems. Some, like King Saul, only turn to God as an emergency relief when they are overwhelmed with problems. It doesn't work like that; it did not work for Saul either. *"And when Saul inquired of the LORD, the LORD did not answer him, either by dreams or by Urim or by the prophets" (1 Samuel 28: 6).* Be acquainted with God when all is well so that you can know how to connect to Him when the enemy comes against you like a flood.

God wants to restore His voice in your life for total transformation. The Bible says, *"The voice of the LORD is over the waters; The God of glory thunders; The LORD is over many waters" (Psalm 29:3).* "The waters" in this verse is a picture of the Bible. Hearing God's voice begins with interacting daily with His Word and developing the habit of listening to Him during meditation and prayer. God will not waste His time speaking to someone who will not obey Him. Do you follow His voice?

Let us pray
1. *Father, thank You for this day and Your voice in my life.*
2. *O Lord, forgive me for disobeying Your voice and choosing my own ways.*
3. *Fire of God, fall on me now and restore the voice of God in my life, in Jesus' name.*
4. *Fire of God, burn away every spiritual wax in my ears and connect me to the realm of revelation, in Jesus' name.*
5. *You evil voices, speaking in my mind, die! In the name of Jesus.*
6. *My Father, amplify Your voice in my life and direct me daily this year, in the name of Jesus.*

Prophetic Prayers of the Week

1. *I will not miss my steps this week. I will be in the right place at the right time, in Jesus' name.*

2. *God's Word in my mouth and my testimony will draw the lost to Jesus Christ this week, in Jesus' name.*

3. *Darkness shall not submerge this nation and frustrate its prophetic destiny. The Church will continue to shine more and more, in Jesus' name.*

| Tuesday 20 May | THE WORD: KEY TO |
| | OPEN DOORS |

Read: Revelation 3:7-8

Bible in 1 year: Psa. 22-24
Bible in 2 years: Psa. 135-136

"Until the time that his word came to pass, The word of the Lord tested him" (Psalm 105:19).

God created everything by the power of His Word, which is the Master key to uncommon open doors (Psalm 33:6). As you engage God's Word this season, He will recreate your damaged destiny.

The Word has the answer to the questions troubling your mind. It has the light you need to brighten your dark path and the counsel you need to solve that complex problem. Several of God's children in the Bible experienced open doors and new beginnings when the Word came to them: (1) The prison door opened for Joseph to regain his freedom when his Word came (Psalm 105:17-25). Are you trapped in any situation? Let whatever you need to be free be released today, in Jesus' name. (2) The door of liberty from captivity for Israel was opened when Daniel found what was written in the book of Prophet Jeremiah (Daniel 9:2; Jeremiah 29:10). The Word you need for your breakthrough is recorded in the Bible. I pray that the Holy Spirit would connect you to it this month, in Jesus' name. (3) Jesus' ministry was launched with power when He found His Word in Isaiah 61:1-3 and Luke 4:16-21. . Do you know that God's glorious future for you is recorded in Scripture? I discovered my picture in the Scripture during a prayer retreat in 1997 and have been pursuing it till date.

How can you engage the Word for your open door?

1. **Seek divine knowledge:** In Luke 11:52, Jesus calls the knowledge of the truth in the Kingdom a key. Diligently seek answers to your problem in the Bible. Sit down and search and you will find the key.

2. **Pray the Word:** Psalm 107:20, *"He sent His word and healed them, And delivered them from their destructions."* God's Word carries His power and presence. Send the Word through your prayer to break barriers and bring restoration in your life and family. The restoration wind began to blow in the valley of dry bones when Ezekiel started to declare the Word of the Lord.

3. **Put the Word to practice:** Begin to do what the Bible says about your situation. Breakthrough will come.

God's Word is key to open doors. Engage it to change your story!

Let us pray

1. *Father, thank You for the Power made available to me through Your Word.*
2. *Father, all I see and what I do not see were created by You; You can recreate my shattered destiny, in Jesus' name.*
3. *Father, send forth Your Word and put an end to this phase of my life, for a new beginning, in Jesus' name.*
4. *Father, illuminate my spirit to capture my Word for open doors this month, in Jesus' name.*

5. *Father, arise and let every evil power that is saying I must end on the way be wiped out, in Jesus' name.*

6. *Father, let uncommon doors open before me as I step out every day this month, in Jesus' name.*

Wednesday 21 May

BECOME AN 11TH HOUR LABOURER

Read: Matthew 20:1-15

Bible in 1 year: Eze. 22-24
Bible in 2 years: Psa. 137-138

"Therefore pray the Lord of the harvest to send out laborers into His harvest" (Matthew 9:38).

God accomplishes His missions with consecrated, dedicated, and diligent men and women. And dedication is the key to distinction.

Today, we are considering the story of the laborers recruited at the 11th hour—5 p.m. While the others started at 9 a.m., they came in 8 hours later. They were recruited late from the marketplace as the last hope squad.

"Marketplace ministry," also called business as ministry, business as mission, or workplace ministry, views secular workplaces as a platform for sharing Jesus' love—the Gospel. It is about Christians serving God through their daily work. Every child of God is called to serve, which is the meaning of ministry. Wherever you work is your place of ministry. Unfortunately, most people think of ministry to mean preaching. A nurse, mechanic, lawyer, teacher, politician, etc. should all work as ministers, revealing Christ to the world through their work. While the pastor, prophet, or apostle is ministering in the church, you should be a minister where you work. How? Serving with integrity and sharing the Gospel when the opportunity presents itself. You may not need to resign from your work to serve God.

67

The most interesting thing about the 11th-hour laborers is that they finished their assignment and brought joy to the master. They satisfied the master's deepest desire, so he ordered the foreman to start the payment with them. And they received the same pay as those who had worked since morning.

The secret to the success of the 11th-hour laborers was: They worked with (1) a sense of privilege, (2) a sense of urgency, (3) a sense of diligence, (4) one agenda to finish the task, (5) they worked without reservations. You can distinguish yourself by following in the steps of the 11th-hour workers.

Let us pray

1. *Father, thank You for the privilege to work with You.*
2. *Father, help me to see my work as a ministry to You and the people I serve, in Jesus' name.*
3. *Father, fill me with Your Spirit and help me to develop the 11th-hour laborer mentality, in Jesus' name.*
4. *Pray through the five secrets of the success of the 11th-hour worker. Let it become your way of work.*
5. *Pray that all believers in this nation will become conscious to do their work as ministry.*

Thursday 22 May   **EVEN IF HE DOES NOT**

Read: Daniel 3:8:24

> **Bible in 1 year:** Eze. 25-27
> **Bible in 2 years:** Psa. 139-140

"If we are thrown into the blazing furnace, the God we serve is able to deliver us from it . . . But even if he does not . . . we will not serve your gods or worship the image of gold you have set up" (Daniel 3:17-18).

God can deliver you from the challenge you are facing now. However, He can decide to do it His way. What will you do if your deliverance tarries? When things became very tough, the three Hebrew boys instead of surrendering to the King's threats boldly declared, *"If we are thrown into the blazing furnace, the God we serve is able to deliver us from it . . . But even if he does not . . . we will not serve your gods or worship the image of gold you have set up" (Daniel 3:17-18).*

Are you facing a threatening situation right now, and does deliverance seem impossible? You must decide what to do, like the three Hebrew boys. You must make up your mind to trust God till death. Why?

1. ***God is All-powerful:*** God can turn any situation around despite opposition. In Isaiah 46:10, He says, *"My purpose will stand and I will do all that I please."* He quenched the flames of fire for the Hebrew boys when they landed in the furnace. What if they had withdrawn their trust in

69

God at the critical moment of being thrown into the fire?

2. **God's presence is always with you:** In Matthew 28:20, Jesus says, *| Surely I am with you always to the very end of the age."* You can trust Him to intervene if He is always with you as promised. Keep trusting Him.

3. **God is love:** God loves you deeply and desires your well-being. He cannot abandon you. Whatever happens will work for you (Romans 8:28). Keep trusting God.

Shadrack and his friends had faith that God could deliver them from the death sentence, but even if God didn't do what they wanted, they were committed to Him. They were confident that He had an excellent plan for them. Can you sincerely say, "I know God can deliver me from this situation, and even if He doesn't, I am wholeheartedly committed to Him"?

Let us pray
1. *Father, thank You because You are Sovereign and there is nothing You cannot do.*
2. *Father, thank You because You know what I am going through now and You have a glorious plan for me, in Jesus' name.*
3. *Father, I commit myself to obey You till the end, no matter what, in Jesus' name.*
4. *Father, deliver me from the fear of the fire, storm, or wilderness of trial, in Jesus' name.*
5. *Father, manifest in my life and cause me to triumph over the situations threatening my life, in Jesus' name.*

6. *Father, I surrender my destiny into Your loving hands and wait for my deliverance, in Jesus' name.*

Friday 23 May

WHAT DO YOU OFFER TO GOD?

Read: Genesis 4:1-5

> **Bible in 1 year:** Eze. 28-30
> **Bible in 2 years:** Psa. 141-142

"So give yourselves completely to God" (James 4:7 NCV).

Giving to God is offering yourself to Him. What you offer to God represents you. Your offering speaks much about you. A lover of God gives the best, like Abel, while a shallow believer gives the rest to God like Cain.

Cain lost the opportunity to excel with God when his offering was rejected. He offered God some vegetables instead of a blood sacrifice like Abel. Many people want to serve God their way, without regard for His requirements. But God will always have His way. We cannot squeeze Him into our mould of compromise and shallow Christianity. You cannot offer God two hours on Sunday morning when He wants your whole life. You cannot tell God you will serve Him only at retirement when He needs you as a youth.

Ministering before God means giving everything. When you come before God, He expects a blood sacrifice from you. In Leviticus 17:11, we are told that the life of a human being is in the blood. God wants your life. Cain came along with some vegetables, but God rejected them. Your life is in jeopardy when God rejects you and your work.

Friend, it is time you reflect on the quality of your commitment to God. Are you offering blood sacrifices or vegetables to God? James 4:7 says, *"So, give yourselves completely to God."* God wants all of you so that all you have can become assets for His Kingdom. You cannot continue to pretend to serve God without doing anything for Him that will cost you. He doesn't want your leftovers. He wants your best and not the rest. From today, decide to go deeper and closer to Jesus Christ. Be willing to give Him all He demands from you. You will become a great blessing to this generation.

Let us pray

1. *Father, thank You for offering Your best on the cross to make me become the best before You.*
2. *Father, forgive me for offering leftovers to You, in Jesus' name.*
3. *Father, help me to give You my life and my best, for Your glory, in Jesus' name.*
4. *Abel gave the best to God, moved by divine love and revelation; Father, please fill my heart with Your love, in Jesus' name.*
5. *Father, there are several vacancies in the vineyard; please pour Your Spirit in the Church and raise genuine laborers for the work of the Gospel, in Jesus' name.*
6. *Father, teach us to serve You according to Your standards and not ours, in Jesus' name.*

Saturday 24 May

BE KIND TO THE POOR

Read: Psalm 41:1-3

> **Bible in 1 year:** Eze. 31-33
> **Bible in 2 years:** Psa. 143-144

"When you give to the poor, it is like lending to the LORD, and the LORD will pay you back" (Proverbs 19:17 GNT).

A generous heart is a precious possession you should cautiously preserve. According to God, poverty is not the lack of things but the inability to share the little you have with those in need. To lose your generosity is to disconnect from God's provision plan. Every time God positions you in a place to give, He is giving you an opportunity to receive His blessing.

One Sunday, a poor man came to Hudson Taylor, who later became a famous missionary, to ask him to pray for his desperately sick wife. When he arrived at their home, Taylor saw that they had nothing to eat or buy medications. With his last coin in his pocket, he knelt to pray for the woman, resisting the voice of the Holy Spirit to give it to the needy family. He later described what happened to him: "But scarcely had I opened my lips with "Our Father who art in heaven," then conscience said, 'Dare you mock God? Dare you to kneel down and call Him Father with that money in your pocket?"

Taylor gave the poor man his last coin, with which he could purchase food and medicine for his sick wife. Taylor returned home with empty pockets but a full heart. The next day, he received an anonymous letter in the mail with some money – four times what he had given away the night before.

Prayer prepares and positions us to express generosity. We should never cover up stinginess with prayer. Apostle James emphasizes that we should demonstrate our love and faith in Jesus Christ through works of generosity. In Chapter 2:15-16, he says, *"Suppose a brother or sister is without clothes and daily food. If one of you says, 'Go in peace; keep warm and well fed,' but does nothing about their physical needs, what good is it?"*

Don't ignore the poor who come to you with needs. You lend to God when you give to them. You will surely be rewarded.

Let us pray
1. *Father, thank You for blessing me with spiritual and physical blessings, in Jesus' name.*
2. *Father, thank You because giving to the poor is investing in You.*
3. *Father, fill my heart with Your love and wisdom, and help me to become a channel of Your blessings to the poor, in Jesus' name.*
4. *Father, show me those I need to help this season, in Jesus' name.*
5. *Father, bless the ministries that care for the poor in this nation, in Jesus' name.*
6. *Father, pour Your rain on me and increase me financially to care for more in need, in Jesus' name.*

Sunday 25 May   **GOD CAN USE**
                                     ANYONE
Read: Joshua 2:1-10

> **Bible in 1 year:** Eze. 34-36
> **Bible in 2 years:** Psa. 145-146

"For the eyes of the LORD range throughout the earth to strengthen those whose hearts are fully committed to him" (2 Chronicle 16:9).

God moves in mysterious ways to perform His miracles amongst men. He can use anyone available to do His work. He is not looking for the qualified; He seeks the available and qualifies them. He can use you if you make yourself available from today. Stop thinking that He uses only some particular people.

Joshua knew the strategies to fight wars. So, he sent two soldiers secretly to spy on the city of Jericho. He knew the disadvantage of sending many soldiers, as recorded in Numbers 13:1-14:4. The Bible records that the two men went into the house of a harlot (Vs. 1). A twenty-first Christian will condemn them for entering into a harlot's house. But God, who knows the future, had directed them there. Rahab risked her life to hide the spies and save them from death. Another citizen of Jericho might have handed them to the authorities. Rahab's house was strategically positioned on the wall, facilitating their escape.

Who would have believed that Rahab would be an instrument in God's hands to accomplish His purpose by facilitating the entry of Israel into the Promised Land? Man

76

quickly condemns, but God knows how to use anything to His glory.

Friend, God wants to use you. So, always ask Him to lead you as you step out daily. He can use anyone around you to perform His will. Also, be available at any time He wants to use you for a task. Stop condemning yourself and submit to the leading of the Holy Spirit.

Often, God uses what seems useless to man to achieve His purpose.

Let us pray

1. *Father, thank You because You can use anyone and You have chosen to use me.*
2. *Father, I hand my heart to You; use me the way You want from today, in Jesus' name.*
3. *Father, position me to rescue some people Satan has targeted for destruction, in Jesus' name.*
4. *Father, position people like Rahab on my path to rescue and preserve me in the day of trouble, in Jesus' name.*
5. *Father, order my steps as I go out daily this month, in Jesus' name.*
6. *Raise your right hand and pray 5 times, "You arrow of destruction and death shut against me, be destroyed by fire, in Jesus' name."*

Monday 26 May   **FAITH IS NOT**
                                     ALWAYS LOGICAL

Read: Hebrews 11:1-16

> **Bible in 1 year:** Eze. 37-39
> **Bible in 2 years:** Psa. 147-148

"Now the just shall live by faith: but if any man draws back, my soul shall have no pleasure in him" (Hebrews 10:38).

I t takes unwavering faith to please God. To walk by faith, you must know that sometimes people will consider you illogical or foolish. Faith does not always agree with human logic. You may miss out on God if you spend time trying to help people understand you instead of obeying God promptly.

Abraham was ninety years old and had stopped having intimacy with Sarah when God told him he was going to have a child. The possibility of him having a child was nil, but he believed God with all his heart. God was so pleased with Abraham because he believed. God gets excited when you believe because *"Without faith, it is impossible to please Him"* *(Hebrews 11:6).*

Reading the Bible, you discover how people looked foolish when they believed God for miracles. Imagine how people ridiculed Noah, who was trying to build an ark to save his family from a flood at a time when there had never been rain in the world. He believed because God had revealed what was going to happen to him. Today, some people laugh at us when we tell them that Jesus Christ is coming back to judge the world.

Friend, do not be afraid of looking odd when you act by faith. After a moment of acting on and declaring your conviction in God's promises, there will be a manifestation of his blessings in your life. Your mockers will be put to shame. So keep exercising your faith. The more you do so, the more you prosper. Don't mind those speaking against you. Ignore them and continue to please God with faith. Your results will shut their mouths.

Let us pray

1. *Father, thank You because You can make anything out of nothing, in Jesus' name.*
2. *Father, thank You because, in Christ, I am a sign and a wonder, in Jesus' name.*
3. *I receive the baptism of courage to exercise my faith, in Jesus' name.*
4. *Father, shine Your light and cause me to see the great things You will do in my life and this generation, in Jesus' name.*
5. *Father, open my eyes like Noah that I may not perish with the wicked, in Jesus' name.*
6. *Father, use me to rescue several lost souls on their way to hell this year, in Jesus' name.*

Prophetic Prayers of the Week

1. *I know what God wants me to do with my life; nothing will stop me from doing His will, in Jesus' name.*
2. *The challenges I am facing now will not ruin me; they will make me stronger, in Jesus' name.*

3. *I receive divine strength and wisdom to accomplish every task I have in my hands this week excellently, in Jesus' name.*

Read: Isaiah 54:1-17

> **Bible in 1 year:** Eze. 40-42
> **Bible in 2 years:** Psa. 149-150

"Do not be afraid—you will not be disgraced again; you will not be humiliated" (Isaiah 54:4 GNT).

S atan has an evil plan to disgrace you. He wants you to finish in shame. But God's agenda concerning you is that you serve Him and finish in glory and honor. He says, *"Do not be afraid – you will not be disgraced…you will not be humiliated."*

Satan has both short and long-term plans against your life or ministry. You must be aware of them and pray to stop him. Sometimes, God reveals demonic attacks that will happen months or years later to prepare us to pray and be alert. In Luke 22:31-34, Jesus informed Peter about Satan's plan to disgrace him by causing him to deny Christ. This was to prepare Peter to stand against it. Unfortunately, Peter, being an immature disciple, did nothing about it. Even at Gethsemane, when Jesus was praying, he was sleeping. He later faced those who came to arrest Jesus with a sword, against God's will, and denied Jesus three times in one night. Disgrace is inevitable when you fail to prepare yourself against the enemy's attacks. Without Jesus' intercession for Peter, he would have ended in disgrace.

Look around carefully; you will see some who were once flourishing financially and who are broke. I know millionaires who have become miserable today. Do you know that Satan wants the same thing to happen to you? So, if you are wealthy and excelling financially today, don't become negligent. Pray that God would establish you and make you unbreakable. There is no wealth that cannot finish.

Some ministers of the Gospel who were very famous in the past today have been silenced and disgraced by the devil. Some got caught up in scandalous affairs, and some are currently in jail. Are you involved in ministry? Never forget that Satan wants to destroy your ministry.

Let us humble ourselves before the Almighty God today and cry out to Him to rescue us from satanic disgrace.

Let us pray
1. *Father, thank You because shame is not my portion in Christ.*
2. *Father, forgive and cleanse me for opening any door to the spirit of disgrace in my life, in Jesus' name.*
3. *Today, I close every door I have opened to the spirit of disgrace, in Jesus' name.*
4. *Father, arise and let my strong enemies be scattered, in Jesus' name.*
5. *Father, arise and let every enemy strategy to trap me into the web of disgrace be scattered, in Jesus' name.*
6. *Father, turn every shame in my life to honor and restore my wasted years, in Jesus' name.*

Wednesday 28 May   **DEVELOP YOUR**
                        SPIRIT

Read: 1 Corinthians 14:1-4

> **Bible in 1 year:** Eze. 43-45
> **Bible in 2 years:** Col. 1-2

"But you, beloved, building up yourselves on your most holy faith, praying in the Holy Spirit" (Jude 20)

Your spiritual strength is a function of how much of God's power you carry in your spirit. Like a battery, you must charge your spirit man by praying in tongues.

Every Christian must develop the art of spending quality time – even hours praying in the Spirit/ in tongues. The Bible says you build up yourself in the faith when you pray in the Holy Spirit. Let me emphasize that praying in the Holy Spirit is the same as praying in tongues. I feel energized and renewed when I pray in tongues for extended periods.

"But you, beloved, BUILDING UP YOURSELVES on your most holy faith, praying in the Holy Spirit" (Jude 20). Pray in tongues for an hour every day for the next month and see what will happen to your spiritual life. I guarantee you a dramatic change if you will do it faithfully. As the Bible says, you will be spiritually charged and built up as you persist in praying in tongues.

1 Corinthians 14:4 says, _"He who speaks in an unknown tongue edifies himself."_ The Word and prayer will cause you to develop in the spirit and become a giant for God's Kingdom.

Today, we have several weak, immature, and barren in God's house because they don't do spiritual exercises. You cannot develop spiritually without training your spirit.

Do you desire to minister with miraculous results? Do you want your gift to touch many more people? I have shown you the secret today. Engage meditation and praying in tongues, consistently and persistently. God's power will break forth mightily in your life. Now that you know, go to work!

Let us pray

1. *Father, thank You for the gift of the Holy Spirit and the gifts in my life.*
2. *Father, I open my heart to You; fill me afresh with the Holy Spirit and give me the gifts I need for Your work, in Jesus' name.*
3. Pray in tongues for long today.

Thursday 29 May　　　　**DON'T BE**
　　　　　　　　　　　　　　　WASTEFUL

Read: John 6:5-13

Bible in 1 year: Eze. 46-48
Bible in 2 years: Col. 3-4

"He said to His disciples, gather up the fragments that remain, that nothing be lost" (John 6:12)

Frugality is a key to prosperity. "Frugality" is being mindful and prudent with your resources, avoiding unnecessary expenses and waste. As a Christian, embracing frugality is a powerful way to live a faithful life while achieving your goals. The law of the Kingdom is that God gives you more when you manage what you have received well. *"Whoever can be trusted with very little can also be trusted with much, and whoever is dishonest with very little will also be dishonest with much" (Luke 16:10).*

In the story of feeding five thousand men with five loaves of bread and two fish, Jesus demonstrated frugality. After the meal, He ordered His disciples to gather all the remains without losing a single crumb. Why would Jesus care about crumbs after God had provided abundantly? Wastefulness and extravagancy are destiny destroyers that must not be tolerated.

Frugality is the most common characteristic of millionaires. They "Count their pennies." They do everything to minimize losses through wastage and stealing. Losses can ruin any business, regardless of its size.

85

Here are five basic rules to kill wastage in your life:

1. ***Prioritize needs over wants:*** Be honest about what you need versus what you want. Some things you buy are not necessary for now. Don't buy a car at the wrong time to look big. Invest your money to grow your capital. Invest in God's work.

2. ***Live simply:*** Refrain from unnecessary luxuries and strive for a life of simplicity and humility. Remember, *"Godliness with contentment is great gain." (1 Timothy 6:6).*

3. ***Save and invest wisely:*** Always save and put your money to work before you spend the profit.

4. ***Avoid debt:*** Work to avoid debt, which can be a significant burden. Instead, focus on living within your means and saving for the future.

5. ***Give generously:*** Frugality is about being a faithful steward. Give generously to support God's work and help those in need.

To achieve great things in life, you must manage your resources effectively.

Let us pray

1. *Lord Jesus Christ, thank You for teaching me that wastefulness is destructive and that You hate it.*
2. *Father, forgive me for wasting resources and opportunities, in Jesus' name.*

3. O Lord, deliver my soul from wastefulness and extravagance, in Jesus' name.

4. Father, fill my heart with the Spirit of wisdom to manage all I have according to Your will, in Jesus' name.

5. Father, help me make all the money I must make, save all I must, and give all I must give in Jesus' name.

6. Father, open my eyes to see opportunities to invest for financial increase, in Jesus' name.

Friday 30 May   **PUT YOUR TRUST IN GOD**

Read: Psalm 118:8-14

> **Bible in 1 year:** Col. 1-2
> **Bible in 2 years:** 1Thess. 1-2

"Do not put your trust in princes, in human beings, who cannot save" (Psalm 146:3)

The worst error you can make is to put your trust in man. You may frustrate your destiny and end up cursing God. It has taken me a long time to learn that I must put my trust only in God and not in any human being. God can use anyone He chooses to help you, but don't trust man. Don't look up to anyone as if your future is lost without them. Never! I cannot count the number of people who made sweet promises to help me but never showed up. Though they didn't keep their word, the faithful God cared for me, and I am here today. I am learning to put my complete trust in Him.

Sometimes, you may be upset because those you expected to help you have let you down. Maybe some of them made promises but did not keep them. So, if you need help from someone, know these:

1. They have their own pressing needs. FEEL FOR THEM!
2. Others have asked for help from them before you. BE PATIENT; they will get to you.
3. They may not have what you want from them at this time. WAIT!

4. They may not be the one God has chosen to solve your problem. DON'T BE MAD AT THEM.
5. They may not be led to help you. DON'T CURSE THEM.
6. They may give you part of what you need. APPRECIATE IT.
7. They may meet your needs. THANK THEM SINCERELY, AND ALSO THANK GOD FOR USING THEM TO HELP YOU.

Never forget this! The person who cannot help you today may be able to help you tomorrow. Take life easy. Sometimes, God does not want certain types of people to help you because they may later seek to manipulate you. I know a lady who received an envelope from a relative while traveling abroad. She told me in frustration that the man did not appreciate anything she gave him. He said he needed a car for the help he gave her. This lady had not yet bought a car for herself. So, sometimes, persevere in lack rather than go for help that would entangle you.

Put your trust in God. He will see you through!

Let us pray

1. *Father, thank You for faithfully supplying all my needs up to this point.*
2. *Father, thank You because You can never leave nor forsake me, in Jesus' name.*
3. *Father, forgive me for trusting people and getting angry at those who did not help me.*
4. *Father, teach me to trust You with all my heart, in Jesus' name.*
5. *Father, release Your angel of breakthrough on my behalf today for a testimony, in Jesus' name.*

6.   *Father, let those You have chosen to help me not miss me, and may You lead me to those You want me to help, in Jesus' name.*

**PAIN CAN MAKE
YOU BETTER OR
BITTER**

Read: Genesis 45:1-11

Bible in 1 year: Col. 3-4
Bible in 2 years: (Catch-up)

"So if you are suffering in a manner that pleases God, keep on doing what is right, and trust your lives to the God who created you, for he will never fail you"
1 Peter 4:19 (NLT).

You can go closer to God when you experience tragedy, disaster, and pain. Unfortunately, troubles turn some people away from God, even when He can help them. Friend, for pain to make you better or bitter, it depends on how you choose to respond to it. So, will you let that experience you are going through now make you bitter, or will you turn to God and let the pain make you better?

Joseph went through a lot of pain in the hands of his brothers. They hated him, sold him into slavery, and because of that he went through several years of torment. The pain could have made Joseph bitter, but our text reveals that his attitude was godly and positive. He chose to love his brothers instead of paying them back in their own coins. He told his brothers, *"But don't be upset, and don't be angry with yourselves for selling me to this place. It was God who sent me here ahead of you to preserve your lives" (vs. 5)*. Joseph had the power

91

to deal with his brothers very severely, but he chose to focus on God's plan.

Focusing on God's plan during trials is crucial for spiritual growth. Do you know that you grow spiritually when you go through hard times? Troubles stretch you spiritually, producing the fruit of the Holy Spirit in you. For example, you cultivate the fruit of patience when things are delayed. You learn to love when people reject and hate you. That is why we say pain can make you better. But it always depends on how you respond to it.

Some Christians erroneously think that it is never God's will for them to suffer. They say if you have any pain in your life, it is due to a lack of faith. 1 Peter 4:19 says, *"So if you are suffering in a manner that pleases God, keep on doing what is right, and trust your lives to the God who created you, for he will never fail you" (1 Peter 4:19 NLT).* Jesus Christ may not immediately remove the situation, but He will accompany you through it. So, whatever you are facing now should draw you closer to Him.

Let us pray
1. *Father, thank You for Your glorious plans in my life, in Jesus' name.*
2. *Father, give me the grace to gain from every painful situation that comes my way, in Jesus' name.*
3. *Father, help me to love those who hate me and manifest the fruit of the Holy Spirit in every trial, in Jesus' name.*
4. *Father, turn the evil men have planned against me around for my good, in Jesus' name.*
5. *Father, let nothing turn me away from my inheritance, in Jesus' name.*

6.   *O Father, cause everything You have committed into my hands to prosper abundantly this year, in Jesus' name.*

=======

Sunday 1 June

**ENTER WITH A
PURE HEART**

Read: James 4:7-10

> **Bible in 1 year:** Mat. 1-4
> **Bible in 2 years:** 1Thess. 3-4

"Blessed are the pure in heart, for they will see God"
(Matthew 5:8).

We need holiness to seek God and enjoy intimate fellowship with Him, for *"Without holiness no one will see the Lord" (Hebrews 12:14).* Holiness is indispensable for closeness with God.

As Jesus said, *"Blessed are the pure in heart, for they will see God" (Matthew 5:8).* I don't believe this verse refers to seeing God in heaven when we die one day. Jesus is talking about seeing God now, in the sense of entering into His presence in a relationship of intimacy so we can know His heart and mind.

What does it mean to be pure in heart? "Pure" means holy. Therefore, Jesus is saying, in effect, "Blessed are the holy in heart, for they will see God." The word "Holy" means to "Sanctify, or set apart." *"Blessed are the [sanctified or set apart] in heart, for they will see God."* When you are pure in heart, your mind is set on God and His ways. *"I am the LORD your God; consecrate yourselves [set yourselves apart] and be holy, because I am holy" (Leviticus 11:44). "I am the LORD, who makes you holy" (Leviticus 20:8).*

94

Perhaps no word describes God better than HOLINESS. God is saying, "Set yourself in the same way that I set myself; be holy, just as I am holy." To consecrate yourself means to position yourself to please the Lord. Leviticus 20:26 says, *"You are to be holy to me because I, the LORD, am holy, and I have set you apart from the nations to be my own."* He saved you to live for Him

Holiness always involves separation. You have to break away from something to focus on God. It may cost you some relationships and certain things you cherish so much. That is the price you must pay to walk with God. You cannot please God when you want to be a men pleaser.

Let us pray
1. *Father, thank You for making me holy through the blood of Jesus Christ.*
2. *Father, thank You for adopting me into Your family through the price Jesus paid on the cross for me.*
3. *Father, shine Your light in our hearts and expose the things that defile us, in Jesus' name.*
4. *Father, teach me how to walk before You in purity, in Jesus' name.*
5. *Father, please remove from my life anything that is hindering my prayer, in Jesus' name.*
6. *Father, deliver me from the trap of displeasing You to people, in Jesus' name.*

Prophetic Prayers of the Week
1. *Father, I thank You because You will put a new song in my mouth to praise You every day this month, in Jesus' name.*

2. *Every satanic gang up against me this month will not prosper, in Jesus' name.*

3. *I am God's vessel set apart for a special purpose; nothing will defile me, in Jesus' name.*

Read: Romans 8:4-5

> **Bible in 1 year:** Mat. 5-7
> **Bible in 2 years:** 1Thess. 5; 2Thess. 1

"If we live in the Spirit, let us also walk in the Spirit"
(Galatians 5:25).

Christianity is life in the Spirit. Believers who operate in God's power know how to relate with the spirit realm.

Did you know that there is a spirit world that is greater than the physical world we inhabit? This physical world is actually an extension of the spirit world. The Bible says, *"God is a Spirit, and those who worship Him must worship in spirit and truth" (John 4:24).* This implies that God created all things, and therefore, there is a spiritual dimension to everything He made. Nothing in the universe is disconnected from Him.

God gave man a physical body to live in while existing in this physical world, which is part of the spiritual world. Note that the earth is not separate from God's realm in the spirit. The picture of Genesis 1:2 makes this clear: *"The earth was without form, and void; and darkness was on the face of the deep. And the Spirit of God was hovering over the face of the waters."* We see here that the Spirit of God incubated over the chaotic mass because God directly connects with the earth. Many, because they don't understand the connection between the

97

spirit realm and the physical world, limit their lives to the physical world.

For every one who is born again, the Bible commands us to walk in the Spirit. How do you walk in the Spirit – connect and operate in the spirit realm? (1) It is walking daily in the light of God's Word. (2) It is walking according to Kingdom principles. (3) It is to become conscious that even though you live in this physical world, you are an integral part of the heavenly realm, which is greater than this world. This consciousness will elevate you above this physical world's elements, failures, frustrations, darkness, and corruption.

Life is spiritual, meaning we exist in two worlds: the physical and spiritual realms. Don't limit yourself to the physical realm just because you live in a body. If you do, you will be a victim of fear and anxiety. If you live in Christ, then you are in the superior realm: *"He who comes from above is above all" (John 3:31)*. Arise and exercise authority over the powers of darkness, diseases, and every opposing internal or external force that wants to frustrate your glorious destiny.

Be conscious of who you are in Christ!

Let us pray

1. *Mighty Father, thank You for giving me a place in Your spiritual family.*
2. *Father, thank You for allowing me to sit with Jesus Christ in the spiritual realm, far above principalities and powers.*
3. *Dear Holy Spirit, help me to be conscious daily of Your presence in me and with me, everywhere I go, in Jesus' name.*
4. *Father, teach me how to walk daily in the light of Your Word, in Jesus' name.*

5. *Father, I submit every area of my life to the power of Your Word. Teach me Kingdom principles, in Jesus' name.*

6. *I break every power of distraction and destruction activated by Satan against me in the name of Jesus.*

Tuesday 3 June   **RECEIVE A**
                                       MIRACLE!

Read: Mark 4:35-41

> **Bible in 1 year:** Matt. 8-11
> **Bible in 2 years:** 2Thess. 2-3

"Thus says the LORD, who makes a way in the sea And a path through the mighty waters" (Isaiah 43:16).

Are you currently facing any challenges? Don't be discouraged. Your miracle is on the way!

Everyone faces some problems at a time in life's journey – no one is immune to problems anywhere in the world. But note that what we call problems are generally mere opportunities to demonstrate God's miraculous power. Do you know that problems are forerunners of miracles? The story of every miracle recorded in the Bible started as a problem. So, problems are miracles in disguise.

We serve a God who knows no impossibility and specializes in converting problems to miracles. While God is waiting to deliver miracles to us, some discouraged people have chosen suicide as an option. Others ignore or seek to drown their problems in drugs or alcohol instead of bringing them to God for permanent solutions.

Motivational writers and speakers encourage us to view problems as challenges, replacing the word "Handicap" with "Physical challenge" and "Addiction" with a "Large appetite for something." Others have even gone so far as to suggest that sin should be viewed as a form of human error. Fornication and adultery are described as having fun.

Beloved, welcome Jesus Christ into your boat today. With Him in your boat, you are moving out of your storm to a testimony. Joseph and Daniel are two outstanding Bible characters whom God moved from problems to promotions. Both of them had the right standing with God and lived every moment of their lives to please Him. That is why God did not forsake them during their trials. He gave each of them supernatural deliverance and turned their seemingly insurmountable problems into opportunities for growth and advancement. He will do the same for you. Receive a miracle, in Jesus' name!

Let us pray
1. *Father, thank You because You are a miracle-working God.*
2. *My Father, turn my problem into a promotion, in Jesus' name.*
3. *By the power in the blood of Jesus, I overcome the spirit of demotion in Jesus' name.*
4. *Every conspiracy and confederacy militating against me, scatter in Jesus' name.*
5. *Angels of promotion and increase manifest in my life by fire, in Jesus' name.*
6. *You evil powers assigned to press down my head, release me now, in Jesus' name.*

Read: Genesis 28:10-22

> **Bible in 1 year:** Matt. 12-15
> **Bible in 2 years:** 1Tim. 1-2

"Surely the LORD is in this place, and I did not know it" (Genesis 28:16).

When was the last time you heard God's voice distinctively? Do you believe that God still speaks to His children today? The fact that some people said, "The Lord told me..." and it never came to pass has caused some people to doubt and despise God's voice. Friend, God still speaks and wants to talk to you directly.

One night, God appeared to Jacob in a dream and said clearly, *"I am with you and will keep you wherever you go, and...bring you back to this land; for I will not leave you until I have done what I have spoken to you."* Then Jacob awoke and said, *"Surely the Lord is in this place, and I did not know it."* And he was afraid and said, *"How awesome is this place! This is none other than the house of God, and this is the gate of heaven" (vv.15-17).* This was the first time he encountered the voice of the God of his fathers. Maybe you have heard about God from others; from today, you will hear Him for yourself.

To hear from God, you must:

1. ***Desire to hear His voice:*** You cannot hear God if you are not interested in knowing Him personally. James 4:8

says, *"Draw near to God and He will draw near to you."* Are you hungry to hear God's voice? That is the first step.

2. **Listen to Him:** Isaiah 28:23 says, *"Listen and hear my voice; pay attention and hear what I say."* To hear God speak to you, you must pay attention and listen. What happens when you try to receive an important phone call in a noisy environment? It is not clear. To receive the message clearly, you must withdraw from the noisy crowd to a quiet place. Do the same to hear God. Go to a quiet place and listen to Him.

3. **Believe that God will speak to you:** Some people think that God speaks to some special people. NO! As a loving Father, He wants to talk to all His children. As parents, we speak to all our children, even the babies who can't talk.

Use the written Word to verify the voice. If it concurs, obey it immediately.

Let us pray

1. *Father, thank You for always wanting to talk to me, in Jesus' name.*
2. *Father, help me to overcome distraction and focus on hearing Your voice, in Jesus' name.*
3. *Father, please remove anything blocking Your voice in my life today, in Jesus' name.*
4. *Father, amplify Your voice in my life and make it clearer to me, in Jesus' name.*
5. *Father, open the heavens over my life and give me access to Kingdom mysteries, in Jesus' name.*

6.   *Father, expose secrets concerning my destiny and that of my family, in Jesus' name.*

GOD WILL
ESTABLISH YOU

Read: Psalm 1:1-6

> **Bible in 1 year:** Matt. 16-19
> **Bible in 2 years:** 1Tim. 3-4

"He shall be like a tree Planted by the rivers of water,
That brings forth its fruit in its season, Whose leaf also
shall not wither; And whatever he does shall prosper"
(Psalm 1:3).

In Christ, God establishes those who embrace Him in
Spirit and truth. Are you that Christian who is going
through a lot and wants to abandon your faith in Christ?
Today's message is for you. God will establish you!

The first verse of Psalm 1 tells us what we must
NOT DO. The second verse tells us what we MUST DO.
The third verse tells us WHAT HAPPENS WHEN WE
OBEY the first two verses. Interestingly, the result is that we
become fruitful in life.

This month, we are trusting God to make us fruitful
and productive on all levels. Today's passage shows you how
God will make you fruitful:

1. *He will plant you by the waters:* The Psalmist likened
   a fruitful life to a tree planted by the rivers of water. The
   term "Rivers of water" refers to an irrigation system. In
   the drylands of the Old Testament, water was scarce –
   especially water from rivers. To water their plants,

105

farmers dug wells and created irrigation systems out of them. A tree planted by an irrigated water system was always watered, no matter the season. You will bear fruit no matter the spiritual, social, or economic climate because God will continuously refresh you with living waters from His Word you drink from daily.

2. **Your leaves will not wither:** The leaves represent your activities. Because God will water you continuously, you will be strengthened to do what He has called you to do. You will not become weary or dry up. When others become weak and faint because of a harsh spiritual, social, or economic season, you will continue to enjoy freshness because God has established you by the rivers of water.

3. **You will bear your fruits in season:** Fruits represent results. Without water, trees cannot bear fruits. As you continue to drink daily from God's Word – living waters- you will not miss your season of harvest – results.

4. **You will prosper in all you do:** When God waters you, you produce results in all areas. This is what God will do in your life this month.

To experience this, give God's Word and prayer the central place it deserves in your life this month.

Let us pray
1. *Father, thank You for bringing me to the season of fruitfulness, in Jesus' name.*

106

2. *Father, as I go into Your Word daily this month, saturate my life with Your living waters, in Jesus' name.*

3. *Father, help me to separate completely from anything that promotes barrenness in my life, in Jesus' name.*

4. *O Father, water me in a new way, and let me bear abundant fruits in all areas this month, in Jesus' name.*

5. *Father, take me to new depths in understanding Your Word and Your will, in Jesus' name.*

6. *Father, water the hearts of people who read this book and turn many to Your will, in Jesus' name.*

Friday 6 June **PERSISTENCE IN YOUR VISION**

Read: Hebrews 10:32-39

Bible in 1 year: Matt. 20-22
Bible in 2 years: 1Tim. 5-6

"We do not want you to become lazy, but to imitate those who through faith and patience inherit what has been promised" (Hebrews 6:12).

Often, God gives you a vision of where He is taking you but not what you will go through to get there. Are you wondering why accomplishing your vision is becoming tough? I read these principles on persistency in one of Dr. Myles Munroe's books. Reflect on them to rekindle your zeal to pursue your vision doggedly.

1) Obstacles will come against you and your vision. You must be persistent if you are going to achieve the vision God has given you.

2) Faithfulness means being true to what you have decided to accomplish and letting nothing stop you.

3) Steadfastness means standing fast or steady in the face of resistance.

4) Courage is the ability to stand up in the face of fear.

5) Fear is a positive thing when it gives birth to courage.

6) Your vision will come to pass despite times of stress, disappointment, and pressure.

7) Every point of resistance to your vision comes to make you wiser, not weaker. All opposition comes to strengthen you, not to stop you.

8) Many lose because they quit when life says no the first time, but persistent people win because they never take no for an answer regarding their visions.

9) Perseverance means "To bear up under pressure."

10) Character is formed by pressure. The purpose of pressure is to get rid of what is not of God and to leave what is pure like gold.

11) There is no stopping for a person who understands that pressure is good for him because pressure is one of the keys to perseverance.

12) Vision always demands a cost.

13) Every true vision will be tested for authenticity.

Let us pray

1. *Father, thank You for bringing me to where I am now, in Jesus' name.*

2. *Father, thank You because You will not leave me until You have finished the good work You have started in my life, in Jesus' name.*

3. *Father, persistence always breaks resistance. Make me a persistent disciple in my walk with You, in Jesus' name.*

4. *Father, give me the heart that never takes a NO from the devil as an answer, in Jesus' name.*

5. *Father, cause the pressure the enemy tries to submit me to to produce unprecedented growth in my life, in Jesus' name.*

6. *By God's grace, I will become all God has called me to become in Christ, in Jesus' name.*

Saturday 7 June   **THE FULLNESS OF TIME**

Read: Galatians 4:1-6

> **Bible in 1 year:** Matt. 23-25
> **Bible in 2 years:** 2Tim. 1-2

"But let patience have its perfect work, that you may be perfect and complete, lacking nothing" (James 1:4).

While it is important to establish deadlines for your goals, you must also be willing to rearrange those deadlines to fit in God's plan. Sometimes, your goals do not align perfectly with God's plan. When the Children of Israel left Egypt, God led them through the Sea and then the wilderness for forty years. The journey of 300 miles that would have taken them two weeks lasted 40 years because of God's plan.

God has timing for everything. So, be assured that the vision He has given you will come at the right time. Our text points out that God sent Jesus to be our Savior about four thousand years after the fall of man. Humanly speaking, that was a long time to wait. But He came just as predicted and at just the right time. The Bible says, *"But when the time had fully come, God sent his Son, born of a woman, born under law, to redeem those under law, that we might receive the full rights of sons. (Galatians 4:4–5).*

As long as you can dream, there is hope. As long as there is hope, there is life. Therefore, you must maintain your dream by patiently waiting for its fulfillment in the fullness of time. James 1:4 says, *"But let patience have its perfect work, that you may be perfect and complete, lacking nothing" (NKJV).*

Others who have gone before us have had their faith tested, which produced patience in them to win the race. Let us do the same. The writer of Hebrews expressed it this way: *Wherefore seeing we also are compassed about with so great a cloud of witnesses, let us lay aside every weight, and the sin which doth so easily beset us, and let us run with patience the race that is set before us" (Hebrews 12:1 KJV).*

Your vision will surely come to pass. Be patient!

Let us pray

1. *Father, thank You for all that has been written in the Bible concerning me, in Jesus' name.*
2. *Father, thank You because even though I have plans for my future, Your plans are better.*
3. *O Lord, help me to discern Your plans and align my goals with them, in Jesus' name.*
4. *O Lord, help me to discern divine timing in all I do, in Jesus' name.*
5. *Father, order my steps and do not permit me to go astray from Your plan, in Jesus' name.*
6. *I decree that I will not miss any plan You have ordained for me this year, in Jesus' name.*

Sunday 8 June **ASK FOR THE HOLY SPIRIT**

Read: Luke 11:1-13

> **Bible in 1 year:** Matt. 26-28
> **Bible in 2 years:** 2Tim. 3-4

"If you then, being evil, know how to give good gifts to your children, how much more will your heavenly Father give the Holy Spirit to those who ask Him!" (Luke 11:13).

Your Christian life would be a disaster without the power of the Holy Spirit. Dear child of God, is your spiritual life like a jigsaw – falling and rising? If so, you need the Holy Spirit's power to live a victorious and fruitful Christian life. Ask God for a fresh baptism of the Holy Spirit this week, and you will receive it!

Jesus did not begin His ministry until He had received the power of the Holy Spirit (Luke 4:14). He instructed the early apostles and disciples not to venture into ministry without the power of the Holy Spirit. In obedience to Jesus' command, they risked their lives to wait in Jerusalem until they were clothed with the power of the Holy Spirit (Luke 24:49; Acts 2:1-4). Do you think we can be faithful disciples and effective Gospel ministers in our time without this divine empowerment?

Why do you absolutely need the Holy Spirit? You need Him as your Helper, Teacher, Guide, and Power. Without the Holy Spirit, you cannot achieve anything of worth in the Kingdom. How amazing is it to know that you do not need to struggle or cut your body like the prophets of Baal to receive the Holy Spirit (1 Kings 18)? You only need to ask in faith, and Jesus clarifies in our text that you will receive (vs. 13).

Three things helped me receive the baptism of the Holy Spirit, the first time on Wednesday, 2 December, 1993. (1) I had fully surrendered my life to Jesus Christ, and I was eating the scriptures every day. (2) I was reading and studying books on the Holy Spirit. (3) I set aside Wednesday to fast and pray for the baptism of the Holy Spirit. I had decided in my heart that I would stop fasting on Wednesdays only when I had received the baptism of the Holy Spirit. Praise God, around midday on the second Wednesday, the heavens opened over my life, and the power of the Holy Spirit came on me and filled me. My life had never been the same since that day. I continuously experience infillings as I seek God in prayer and meditation daily.

Are you thirsty for the baptism of the Holy Spirit? Go before God today and ask; you will receive the Holy Spirit and power.

Let us pray
1.   *Father, I thank You for the gift of the Holy Spirit You have given to the Church.*
2.   *Dear Father, fill me with the Holy Spirit today to overflow, in Jesus' name.*
3.   *Lay your hand on your head and pray 7 times, "I receive the baptism of the Holy Spirit now, in Jesus' name."*
4.   *Father, release the gifts of the Holy Spirit I need in my life, in the name of Jesus.*

113

5. *Ask for any gifts you desire and believe that the generous God will give you.*
6. *Lay your hand on your head and pray 7 times, "O mantle of divine power, fall on me now, in the name of Jesus." Spend time and pray in tongues if you can.*

Monday 9 June   **ANSWER SOFTLY**

Read: 1 Kings 12:3-16

> **Bible in 1 year:** Heb. 1-4
> **Bible in 2 years:** Titus 1-2

"A soft answer turns away wrath, But a harsh word stirs up anger. The tongue of the wise uses knowledge rightly, But the mouth of fools pours forth foolishness" (Proverbs 15:1-2).

S oft answers are more potent than harsh words. We win people over more easily when we respond to them tenderly and clearly, rather than shouting and threatening.

Research was recently conducted at Kenyon College among naval personnel. They wanted to evaluate how the tone in which orders were given impacted the response those orders received. The study showed that how the orders were given had a more significant impact on the recipients than the content of the orders. The tone of the orders determined the response.

When someone received an order in a soft voice, the answer tended to be given softly. But when the order was shouted, the response tended to be sharp as well. Interestingly, these findings held true regardless of whether the communication was in person or over the phone. It was not so much the facial expression or body language as the tone and volume of the voice that drove the response.

The same principle applies in our lives, as we see spelled out in Scripture. When we speak to those around us in a harsh, loud, or angry voice, we should expect a negative response. Wisdom must, therefore, guide us in governing the way we speak to others. If you continue to use harsh words, your servant may one day damn the consequences and insult you well before quitting the job.

If you have to correct someone, it should be done in kindness and love rather than harshness. The Bible shows that Jesus was never soft when confronting sin; yet, those who heard Him marveled at the "Gracious words that proceeded out of His mouth" (Luke 4:22).

Rehoboam failed as a leader and lost the kingdom because he spoke harshly to the people. Always decide to respond to people with kindness to save your marriage, career, and ministry.

Let us pray

1. *Father, thank You because Your Words heal and not hurt.*
2. *Father, heal my heart of deep hurts and fill it with divine love, in Jesus' name.*
3. *Father, forgive me for hurting others and myself with harsh words, in Jesus' name.*
4. *Father, fill me with humility and teach me to speak as Jesus Christ did.*
5. *Father, restore every relationship I have destroyed through harsh words, in Jesus' name.*
6. *Father, help me to treat everybody with the respect they deserve from me, in Jesus' name.*

Prophetic Prayers of the Week

1. *Father, thank You because You will strengthen my hands to dismantle the strongholds of my enemies, in Jesus' name.*
2. *God's oil of favor is on my head; I will excel everywhere I go this month, in Jesus' name.*
3. *The kingdom of darkness will not put out my light. I will shine daily this month, in Jesus' name.*

Tuesday 10 June   **PRAYER: KEY TO**
                             RESTORATION

Read: Numbers 21:4-9

> **Bible in 1 year:** Heb. 5-7
> **Bible in 2 years:** Titus 3; Philemon

*"The people came to Moses and said, 'We sinned . . .
Now pray to the LORD to take these snakes away.' So
Moses prayed." (Numbers 21:7 GNT).*

Prayer is a primary key to recovery and restoration. If things have fallen apart in your life, and you want to bounce back, you must involve God through sincere prayer. Healing from hurts, victory over bad habits, and breakthroughs begin to happen when you start praying fervently. Unfortunately, many people try to seek recovery and restoration without involving God through prayer. This is impossible because there is no lasting positive change without God.

After God had rescued the Israelites from Egypt, they were delayed for 40 years in getting to the Promised Land. This delay was their fault. They didn't like where they were, and they didn't like the food – the mana that God had provided for them. The Bible says, *"The people were very discouraged; they began to murmur against God and to complain against Moses" (Numbers 21:4-5 TLB).* They could have taken their problems to God in prayer. Instead, they turned against Moses and God. Consequently, God sent poisonous snakes, and many people got bitten and became sick. The Israelites knew the only solution was to ask Moses to pray for them, and he did. Then, God gave Moses a plan. *"Make a snake image and mount it on a pole. When anyone who is bitten looks at it, he will recover"* *(Numbers 21:8 CSB)*. And the people who looked at the image recovered from the snake bites.

God is a God of recovery. In fact, Jesus' entire mission was— and is —a search and rescue mission. Luke 19:10 says, *"For the Son of Man came to seek and save those who are lost."* Are you struggling with a spiritual, financial, or marital crisis and feeling like you're sinking daily? Friend, it is not over. You can confront your situation like David. *"I waited patiently for the Lord to help me, and he turned to me and heard my cry. He lifted me out of the pit of despair, out of the mud and the mire. He set my feet on solid ground and steadied me as I walked along"* *(Psalm 40:1-2 NLT)*. David was in a tight corner, almost crushed by his enemies. But his prayer to God rescued him. God will save and restore you as you pray.

Let us pray

1. *Father, thank You because You are the God of recovery and restoration; You will restore me, in Jesus' name.*
2. *O Merciful God, remember me today and rescue me from the pit of destruction, disaster, and death, in Jesus' name.*
3. *Father, without You, I am finished; arise and save me from my strong enemies, in Jesus' name.*
4. *Mighty Father, arise and let the forces of darkness mobilized against me be scattered, in Jesus' name.*
5. *Father, let Your hand lift me beyond my capacity, in Jesus' name.*
6. *Father, release the anointing for total recovery and restoration in my life, in Jesus' name.*

Wednesday 11 June   **HUMILTY: KEY TO**
                              HEALTHY
                              RELATIONSHIPS

Read: Philippians 2:1-11

> **Bible in 1 year:** Heb. 8-10
> **Bible in 2 years:** Prov. 1-2

"Be humble, thinking of others as better than yourselves. . . . You must have the same attitude that Christ Jesus had. Though he was God, he did not think of equality with God as something to cling to" Philippians 2:3, 5-6 (NLT).

Humility is key to building and maintaining healthy relationships in the family and society. Pride and arrogance break relationships. Anytime two people fall apart, there is an element of pride that contributed to it. Marriages, families, and Churches are tearing apart because of the spirit of pride. God wants us to follow the path of humility revealed to us by Jesus Christ, which helps us build healthy relationships.

What is "Humility?" It is when you honor others above yourself instead of demanding or clinging to your rights. Philippians 2:3 says, *"Be humble, thinking of others as better than yourselves" (NLT)*. Humility is not a title or a sermon; it is a way of life. There are humble people around us whose Christlikeness shines continuously. We ought to imitate them (1 Corinthians 11:1).

"Pride," on the other hand, makes you critical, judgmental, competitive, stubborn, and unforgiving.

Proverbs 16:18 says, *"Pride leads to destruction; a proud attitude brings ruin" (NCV)*. Pride is also self-deceiving. Most people who are ruled by the spirit of pride are unaware of it, but those around them can see its fruits. What are some of the signs of pride in a relationship? (1) You always give advice but never ask for it. (2) You always prove that you are tough. You don't admit your weaknesses and limitations. (3) You are always right. (4) You don't tolerate the weaknesses of others. You can't build healthy relationships with such an attitude.

1 Peter 3:8 illustrates how humility can enrich our relationships. *"Live in harmony, be sympathetic, love each other, have compassion, and be humble" (GW)*. Humility is the foundation of living in harmony, love, compassion, and sympathy. You become humbler when you spend time with someone who is humble. Do you want to grow in humility? Spend time with Jesus Christ in His Word and in prayer.

Let us pray

1. *Father, thank You for giving me Jesus Christ as a model to follow daily.*
2. *Father, I admit my pride and I bring my heart to You for healing, in Jesus' name.*
3. *Father, teach me to value and treat others as they deserve it, in Jesus' name.*
4. *Father, expose the spirit of pride in my life and help me to deal with it, in Jesus' name.*
5. *Father, teach me how to lift others above myself and celebrate them, in Jesus' name.*
6. *Father, restore to me whatever I have lost through pride, in Jesus' name.*

Thursday 12 June   **ASK FOR DIVINE**
                              DIRECTION

Read: Proverbs 3:5-6

Bible in 1 year: Heb. 11-13
Bible in 2 years: Prov. 3-4

"Commit thy way unto the LORD; trust also in him; and he shall bring it to pass" (Psalm 37:5).

To enjoy divine direction, you must involve God in ALL YOU DO. You must condition your heart to accept and submit to His suggestion concerning every step you make, whether you like it or not.

Divine guidance is an indispensable asset to you as God's child. This is because hearing God increases speed and accuracy in life. Light is key to flight. Not to hear God is to walk in spiritual darkness, which leads to delay, deviation, and destruction. The prodigal son sought independence from his father and drifted far from his voice. He lost everything because he no longer had access to his father's instructing and guiding voice (See Luke 15).

The spiritual posture that enhances hearing or receiving from God is committing your steps to the Lord. The Psalmist says, *"Commit everything you do to the Lord. Trust him to help you do it, and he will" (Psalm 37:5 TLB).* Do not trust your brain or friends to give you the best direction. Human wisdom is limited.

Our text says, IN ALL THE THINGS YOU DO, ACKNOWLEDGE GOD, and He will direct your path. This means that you should not take important steps or make crucial moves in life without consulting the Lord for direction. Do not make significant business, marriage, career, and relocation decisions without seeking God's will. These days, I see young men proposing to Christian ladies in public, expecting them to answer yes on the spot. I keep asking myself, "When does the girl consult God before accepting to marry the brother?" Marriage is not something we handle lightly.

If you have a business deal or a serious decision to make, go to your prayer closet and dialogue with God about it (Isaiah 1:18). If He gives you the green light, proceed, but if you have no peace in your heart, be cautious – don't move. God will not bless the project if you go against His will. Commit your steps to God; He will direct you.

Let us pray

1. *Father, I worship You, my Rock, my Defender, and my Shepherd.*
2. *I commit my ways and plans into Your hands; guide my steps from today, in Jesus' name.*
3. *Father, deliver my soul from the trap of self-sufficiency in Jesus' name.*
4. *Father, instruct, teach, and guide me in the way I should go, in Jesus' name.*
5. *Father, release Your power on me, and let my channels of revelation open up, in Jesus' name.*
6. *Father, let integrity guard my heart and rescue me from perversity, in Jesus' name.*

Friday 13 June

NOT YET TIME TO DIE!

Read: Exodus 23:23-26

Bible in 1 year: Num. 1-3
Bible in 2 years: Prov. 5-6

"I will give you a full life span" (Exodus 23:26b) NIV.

One of Satan's greatest threats against us is, "You will die!" I have received several people who told me, "Pastor, I dreamt and saw you dead." Some of them are in the grave today, but I am still alive, preaching the Gospel. Listen, you will not die now! It is not yet your time to go.

God has assigned a number of days for you to live on this earth, called "Your full life span." King David had a revelation about this and said, "*All the days ordained for me were written in your book before one of them came to be*" *(Psalm 139:16)*. Premature death means to die before the days God has assigned for you. Jesus Christ said, *"I have come--In the volume of the book it is written of Me--To do Your will, O God"* *(Hebrews 10:7)*. He died at thirty-three and a half years old. Can we say He died prematurely? No. He died after fulfilling His destiny. Therefore, no power is permitted to cut your life short until you fulfill your destiny in Jesus' name.

The Bible clarifies that God, by His sovereignty, has the final say concerning your life span – to cut it short or add it. David, who escaped premature death several times, said, "*The Lord has punished me but not handed me over to death*" *(Psalm 118:18)*. It doesn't matter what you go through; death can

125

only take your life away when God hands you over. Death is powerless against you until God does so. Learn to pray like David, *"O my God, Do not take me away amid my days; Your years are throughout all generations" (Psalm 102:24).*

You have an important role to play in fulfilling your days. The Bible says, *"The fear of the LORD prolongs days, But the years of the wicked will be shortened" (Proverbs 10:27).* Sin shortens one's days. I know many young people who died prematurely through reckless living. Years ago, a drunk friend fell from a bridge and drowned in a river. The Word of God can preserve the lives of those who stick to it. *"My son, do not forget my teaching, but keep my commands in your heart, for they will prolong your life many years and bring you prosperity" (Proverbs 3:1-2).*

Jesus died young that you would live long!

Let us pray

1. *Father, thank You for the gift of eternal life and divine health in my life.*
2. *Every yoke of any bad habit working against my health be exposed and broken in the name of Jesus.*
3. *Father, grant me the grace to control my appetite to maintain sound health from now henceforth, in the name of Jesus.*
4. *Every poison of death working in my life, die, in the name of Jesus.*
5. *You power of death and destruction released or programmed against me this year, scatter, in the name of Jesus.*
6. *Fire of God, fall and consume all the agents of darkness in this land who prosper by shedding the blood of the innocent, in the mighty name of Jesus.*

Saturday 14 June **KEYS TO ACCESSING DIVINE LIGHT**

Read: 1 Corinthians 2:9-12

Bible in 1 year: Exo. 14-17
Bible in 2 years: Prov. 7-8

"What no eye has seen, what no ear has heard, and what no human mind has conceived – the things God has prepared for those who love Him" (1 Corinthians 2:9).

Lovers of God enjoy divine light. Light or insight is indispensable for the fulfillment of your destiny. It has been established that you can't become what God wants you to be without revelation. Proverbs 29:18 says, *"Where there is no revelation, people cast off restraint."* In other words, "Where divine revelation is absent, people break rules and live anyhow." The result of living waywardly is always regression and regrets.

What are the keys to accessing light?

1. **God's love:** 1 Corinthians 2:9 says, *"What no eye has seen, what no ear has heard, and what no human mind has conceived – the things God has prepared for those who love Him."* Lovers of God enjoy divine light. Your affection for God is expressed in time spent with Him and the sacrifices you make for Him. Friend, if you genuinely love God, you know, people know, and the devil also knows. Anything that kills your passion for God poisons your spiritual life. Can you be described as a lover of God?

127

2. **Desperation for light:** Hosea 6:3 says, *"Let us know, let us pursue the knowledge of the LORD. His going forth is established as the morning; He will come to us like the rain, Like the latter and the former rain to the earth."* Desperation is a secret of access to divine light. As long as you are hungry for knowledge, you will seek. And when you seek, you will know. For example, you can become desperate to know the keys to success in ministry, soul winning, finances, health, career success, etc. This desperation will open you to divine light as you pray and read to gain understanding. Unfortunately, some people only wish their condition would change but are doing nothing to see it happen.

Dear friend, are you a lover of God? Are you desperate to know Him and His ways? Your love for God and desperation for divine light will open the door of revelation in your life. Revelation will take you to the realm of great possibilities, in Jesus' name.

Let us pray

1. *Father, thank You because You have an answer to every question and a solution to every problem, in Jesus' name.*
2. *O Father, thank You because the things that defy me and easy for You; You will help, in Jesus' name.*
3. *O Father of Light, shine Your light on me and cause my destiny to be illuminated, in Jesus' name.*
4. *Father, arise and turn every darkness in any area of my life to light, in Jesus' name.*
5. *Father, there are truths I must know this year to move to my next level; help me to access them, in Jesus' name.*

6. *O God of revelation, come like rain and change us this season, in Jesus' name.*

Sunday 15 June　　　　　**UNDERSTANDING**
　　　　　　　　　　　　　　　GRACE AND WORKS

Read: Ephesians 2:8-10

> **Bible in 1 year:** Exo. 18-20
> **Bible in 2 years:** Prov. 9-10

"As it is written, there is none righteous, no not one"
(Romans 3:10).

The Bible explicitly clarifies that our works do not save us. We are not going to heaven because of our good works, nor are we saved from hell because of our good works. We are saved by grace through faith in Jesus Christ (vs. 8).

Our salvation is from the Lord. Friend, you cannot do anything to earn it. You cannot be good enough to qualify for heaven. Sometimes, when we go out to evangelize, we meet people who tell us, "I am a good person. I have not done any evil, I have not killed someone." To them to sin is to commit murder. We are sinners because we have been contaminated by Adam's sin (Romans 3:23, 5:12). Your works can never qualify you for heaven. Isaiah 64:6 says, *"But we are all like an unclean thing, And all our righteousness are like filthy rags; We all fade as a leaf, And our iniquities, like the wind."*

But notice that Ephesians 2:8-9, which talks about "Salvation not by works," says we have been "Created for good works." This means that after we are saved, we are supposed to begin to do the good works that Christ has prepared for us. Many Christians ignorant of this truth are not involved in God's work because they think they are saved by grace and not by works. They believe all they have to do is to sit back, relax, and enjoy a smooth ride to heaven.

Friend, do you know that when you meet Jesus Christ one day, he will ask you, "Did you do the things I asked you to do?" "Did you do the good works I ordained you for?" The time is short. So, take advantage of every opportunity now and do God's work. When you die, all you are building now for yourself will not count before God. Work for God!

Let us pray
1. *Father, thank You for saving me from hell and destruction by Your grace.*
2. *Father, You saved me for a purpose; help me to understand it clearly, in Jesus' name.*
3. *Father, some people need to be saved through my labor; give me the grace to labor for souls, in Jesus' name.*
4. *Father, please touch the hearts of my unsaved family members and turn them to Jesus Christ.*
5. *Father, let the grace to serve You come abundantly upon all reading this book today, in Jesus' name.*
6. *Father, pour Your Spirit and call missionaries to take the Gospel to the unreached people groups of Cameroon and the world, in Jesus' name.*

Monday 16 June   DESTINY DEMANDS
                                       DILIGENCE

Read: Luke 18:1-8

> **Bible in 1 year:** Exo. 21-24
> **Bible in 2 years:** Prov. 11-12

"So, we continued the work with half the men holding spears, from first light of dawn till the stars came out" (Nehemiah 4:21).

Your destiny demands rugged diligence to accomplish it. Without diligence, there are levels you cannot attain in life. Friend, if you're going to quit after facing a few challenges and obstacles, you'll never win.

Persistence is withstanding all opposition and forging on by faith – counting on God. Nehemiah could have stopped his work on the wall of Jerusalem due to all the problems, slander, and jeers, but he remained persistent. He was determined to complete his vision. You will never accomplish your vision unless you have the spirit of persistence.

Persistence means that you persist in pursuing what you are after. You stand up against resistance until you wear it out. You make the people who are against to labor until they wear out and leave you alone or become your friends. Friend, I am convinced that you want to realize what God has put in your heart. You will not stop until you get there.

How desperate are you to see your vision materialize? Jesus told a parable in Luke 18 about a persistent woman. She tirelessly appealed to the judge with her request for justice until he said, *"Give it to her!" (See Luke 18:2–8.)* God wants you to do the same. He wants you to claim what He has given you in Christ. Tell life, "This belongs to me." If life refuses, go back and say the same thing every day until it eventually says, "Here, take it!"

Many people lose because they quit when Life says no the first time, but persistent people win because they refuse to back out. They never take no for an answer until they see their vision fulfilled.

Do you have a vision? You will undoubtedly face opposition at some point. Don't give up. Press on until your dream comes true.

Let us pray
1. *Father, thank You because You will never leave me until You have helped me fulfill my divine visions.*
2. *Father, forgive me for yielding to fear and attempting to quit my vision.*
3. *Father, baptize my heart with unquenchable resilience to persist in my vision, in Jesus' name.*
4. *Father, arise and let the Sanballats and Tobias that are fighting my vision be scattered, in Jesus' name.*
5. *Father, give me the grace to finish every good work I have started, in Jesus' name.*
6. *Father, open my eyes to see beyond the challenges I am facing concerning my vision now, in Jesus' name.*

Prophetic Prayers of the Week

1. *Father, thank You because You are the righteous Judge. My case shall be settled this month, in Jesus' name.*

2. *God's fire is burning in my life; I am secured, in the mighty name of Jesus.*

3. *Thoughts of failure, disappointment, unbelief, strange dreams, and fear, have no power over my mind again, in the name of Jesus.*

Tuesday 17 June   **YOU ARE A WARRIOR**

Read: 2 Timothy 2:1-4

Bible in 1 year: Exo. 25-27
Bible in 2 years: Prov. 13-14

"They overcame [Satan] by the blood of the Lamb and by the word of their testimony" (Revelation 12:11).

We know we are warriors because the Bible calls us soldiers (2 Timothy 2:3). Beloved in Christ, you are a spiritual warrior. You are part of God's conquering army on earth at this time.

Ephesians 6:12 describes us as those who "Wrestle." This is because we are constantly involved in spiritual conflicts with the forces of darkness. If God didn't want you to fight, He would have eliminated the devil and all the demons. Our main verse says, *"They overcame [Satan] by the blood of the Lamb and by the word of their testimony" (Revelation 12:11).* Some people don't have a testimony of their victory over satanic forces. They tell you, "I went through the fire, and I got burned. I went under the water and almost drowned." Others tell you they have never smelled the devil. You cannot live right for God and not be confronted by devils. Though a radically consecrated and devoted servant of God, Apostle Paul faced several spiritual attacks. In 1 Thessalonians 2:18, he says, *"For we wanted to come to you – I Paul, tried again and again – but Satan obstructed us."*

The battles against the Kingdom of darkness can sometimes be very tough, but God promises to stay with us all through. Jesus said, *"I am with you always, to the very end of age"* (Matthew 28:20). *"Who shall separate us from the love of Christ? Shall trouble or hardship or persecution or famine or nakedness or danger or sword?...No, in all these things we are more than conquerors through Him who loved us [and called us and gave us our visions]* (Romans 8:35, 37). You are God's investment, and nothing can quench His light in you. Are you facing some battles right now? You will emerge with a great testimony.

Let us pray

1. *Father, thank You for the light of Your Spirit within me, in Jesus' name.*
2. *Father, thank You for equipping me to live as a soldier of the cross, in Jesus' name.*
3. *Father, renew my strength to fight and win every battle I face this year, in Jesus' name.*
4. *Father, give me victory over my strong enemies today, in Jesus' name.*
5. *Father, please cause that every challenge I face this year should make me stronger for You, in Jesus' name.*
6. *Father, arise in my life and let every evil power that does not want me to emerge be submerged, in Jesus' name.*

HOW TO POSSESS A PROMISE

Read: Romans 4:17-21

> **Bible in 1 year:** Exo. 28-31
> **Bible in 2 years:** Prov. 15-16

"For you need endurance, so that after you have done the will of God, you may receive the promise" (Hebrews 10:36).

God has never failed to fulfil any of His promises because He has all it takes to do anything He has said He would do. *"There has not failed one word of all His good promise" (1 Kings 8:56).* You can trust Him concerning any promise He has given you. He will not become a liar in your situation. Do these to possess your promise:

1. **Personalize the promise:** God gives us divine promises in diverse ways. For example, through visions, the written word, or the voice of the Holy Spirit in your heart. When you personalize the Word and it becomes flesh in you, the Holy Spirit causes it to materialize in your life. To personalize the Word, you have to read it prayerfully, meditate on it, and confess it repeatedly until it sinks into your spirit, man.

2. **Exercise faith:** God fulfilled the promise of Isaac because Abraham had strong faith despite all the discouraging factors surrounding the promise. *"And not being weak in faith, he did not consider his own body, already dead*

(since he was about a hundred years old), and the deadness of Sarah's womb. He did not waver at the promise of God through unbelief but was strengthened in faith, giving glory to God" (Romans 4:19-20). The Bible says, *"But was strengthened in faith."* If your faith is not strong, you might never possess the promise. So, strengthen your faith by reading books and listening to faith-building messages.

3. **Glorify God:** The Bible says about Abraham, *"giving glory to God."* Can you begin to praise and worship God now concerning the promise He has given you even though it has not yet materialized? You can do this because you are convinced that He cannot lie.

God's promises in your life will not fail in Jesus' name. Continue to wait in faith, not in fear. Remember that waiting is not wasting. Faith that is not tested is fake. God will show up at the right time. When He steps in, your case becomes a testimony.

Let us pray
1. *Father, I thank You for this day and all Your good promises in my life, in Jesus' name.*
2. *Father, purge me of every spirit of doubt and unbelief, in Jesus' name.*
3. *Father, baptize me with the Spirit of faith and open my eyes to see the good things You have prepared for my future.*
4. *I bind and cast out of my life every spirit of the fear of the future, in Jesus' name.*
5. *Father, please, let me not die until I see my Isaac, in Jesus' name.*
6. *Father, I celebrate You for the victory in my life, in Jesus' name.*

Thursday 19 June   **KEYS TO DOMINATE IMMORALITY**

Read: 1 Corinthians 6:12-20

Bible in 1 year: Exo. 32-24
Bible in 2 years: Prov. 17-18

"Run from sexual sin! No other sin so clearly affects the body as this one does. For sexual immorality is a sin against your own body" (1 Corinthians 6:18).

The "Sex drive" is a flame God has placed in us, to enhance connection and bonding in married couples. Therefore, sexual union in the scope of marriage is a legitimate use of the flame for the purpose for which God created it. Any act of sexual immorality is an abuse of divine order. Those who do it burn themselves, leaving long lasting scars. These could be a venereal disease, a child born out of wedlock, or memories of the relationship that pursue an individual for a life time. Sexual perversion doesn't only destroy the actors, it pollutes the society at large.

What you ought to know about the "Sex drive" is that it can be controlled like we do with fire in our homes. Several households use fire without burning down the house. And this is because they have learned to strictly control the fire for benefit and not destruction.

How can you effectively dominate your sex drive, to live a morally pure life before the Lord? Our text has four rules that can help us:

1. **Know that you are not made for immorality:** Your body was not designed to be a slave to immoral desires and practices. *"But you can't say that our bodies were made for sexual immorality. They were made for the Lord, and the Lord cares about our bodies" (vs. 13).* This implies that you are not obliged to commit sin because of the sex drive that is in you. You can always say no to it if you want.

2. **Know that the power of resurrection is at work in you:** Every born-again Christian is indwelled by the power of resurrection, and this force is stronger than the flame of lust. You have to be conscious of this truth, to dominate immorality. *"And God both raised up the Lord and will also raise us up by His power" (Vs. 14).* Expect to overcome sexual temptation whenever it comes your way

3. **Be conscious that you are Christ's body:** He has redeemed your body for Himself. The consciousness that your body belongs to Christ and deserves to be preserved pure, will save you from immorality. *"Don't you realize that your body is the temple of the Holy Spirit, who lives in you and was given to you by God? You do not belong to yourself" (Vs. 19).*

4. **Flee immorality!** Running away from the temptation of immorality is a command to every one of us. *"Run from sexual sin! No other sin so clearly affects the body as this one does. For sexual immorality is a sin against your own body" (Vs. 18).* Run away from any situation or location that can make you vulnerable to immorality.

Are you battling with any form of immorality? Come before the Lord today in repentance. He will forgive and set you free. Also scrupulously apply this word to your life for victory to last.

Let us pray

1. *Father, thank You for choosing me as Your temple and dwelling place.*
2. *Father, forgive me for tolerating the sin of immorality and perversion in my life.*
3. *O Father, release the blood of Jesus Christ for cleansing in my life, in Jesus' name.*
4. *Fire of God, purge my soul, body, and spirit of all the contaminations of immorality.*
5. *Father, let the flame of divine love rule my heart and strengthen me against immorality.*
6. *I bind every spirit of immorality that is working against me, and I break every yoke of impurity over my spirit, in Jesus' name.*

Friday 20 June   **JESUS HEALS YOU NOW**

Read: Matthew 4:23-25

> **Bible in 1 year:** Exo. 35-37
> **Bible in 2 years:** Prov. 19-20

"And He came down with them and stood on a level place with a crowd of His disciples and a great multitude of people from all Judea and Jerusalem, and from the seacoast of Tyre and Sidon, WHO CAME TO HEAR HIM AND BE HEALED OF THEIR DISEASES…And they were healed" (Luke 6:17-18).

Everywhere Jesus went, He healed ALL. Matthew 4:24 affirms this: *"And they brought to Him all sick people who were afflicted with various diseases and torments, and those who were demon-possessed, epileptics, and paralytics; and He healed them."*

In the medical profession, every doctor specializes in a specific area of medicine. We have ophthalmologists, gynecologists, pediatricians, neurologists, dentists, and so on. In Matthew 9:12, Jesus declares Himself as the Great Physician – a combination of all the specialties. He proved it by healing all the sicknesses that were brought to Him. He healed the deaf, dumb, epileptic, insane, paralytic, etc. He even raised the dead. Why? He is the Great Physician – the Doctor of doctors who cannot refer a case. This Jesus of Nazareth is still healing all sicknesses and setting free captives. This implies there is hope for you. This is the good news of the Gospel.

Many people do not receive healing because they have not heard the Word. Luke 6:17 reveals that it is the Word that comes first, and then healing follows. As you eat the Word from this book daily this month, divine healing and health will break forth in your life. Whenever you receive God's Word and believe it, it becomes power for healing in you. Paul says, *"For I am not ashamed of the gospel of Christ, for it is the power of God ..."* *(Romans 1:16)*. So, meditate on the Word and memorize it.

What is it that the doctors have said concerning you? Have they told you your case is hopeless? Then, they have referred you to the Great Physician – Jesus Christ. He will not send you away or refer you to anyone because all things are possible with Him. Receive your healing now, in Jesus' name.

Let us pray

1. *Father, thank You for the healing power available in Your Word and the name of Jesus.*
2. *Father, I come to You today trusting You for a miracle because all things are possible with You.*
3. *Lord Jesus Christ, no one came to You sick and went away frustrated; visit me and change my story.*
4. *Place your hand on your belly and pray 7 times, "You seed of sickness in me, die now, in Jesus' name."*
5. *Anoint yourself or that sick person and declare total healing and health.*
6. *Father, let Your hand come on every area of my life for total restoration, in Jesus' name.*

Saturday 21 June **BATTLING WITH REJECTION?**

Read: Genesis 37:17-20

> **Bible in 1 year:** Exo. 38-40
> **Bible in 2 years:** Prov. 21-22

Think how much the Father loves us" (1 John 3:1 CEV).

Are you being tormented by the spirit of rejection because of hurts incurred from abuse and abandonment? There is hope for you in God's love. Today, let us expose the spirit of rejection and break its grip over your soul, in Jesus' name.

When you struggle with the spirit of rejection, you experience the following:

1. **Perfectionism:** You are always trying to please everybody perfectly. Unfortunately, it doesn't work because people's needs and expectations vary so much that it's impossible to make everybody happy.

2. **You settle for less:** You accommodate neglect and abuse because you think it is what you deserve. When you don't value yourself because of the distorted image of yourself you have, you become vulnerable to manipulations, abuse, and exploitation. You are created in God's image, and you are a prince/princess in His Kingdom (Psalm139:14; 1 Peter 2:9). Don't settle for the rest, go for the best!

3. ***Becoming aggressive:*** Abuse and neglect leave one with emotional wounds, causing the victim to become hyper-sensitive to hurts. They are aggressive because they are unconsciously trying to protect themselves. They don't want to be vulnerable.

4. ***Isolation:*** The wounds incurred from abuse and abandonment cause the victim to shut off from others. They think, "I don't need others. I can handle it." This position leaves them in frustration because their physical, spiritual, and emotional needs cannot be met in isolation.

5. ***Vowing not to trust people again:*** This may sound logical, but by closing people out, you close yourself in, and your relationships suffer.

6. ***You attract the wrong people:*** The spirit of rejection attracts the wrong people into your life. Why? If you behave with a negative and diminished sense of self-worth, you will keep attracting the wrong people. You are God's child. Walk around overshadowed with the beauty of His glory. You will attract the right kind of people.

Friend, if this word has exposed the spirit of rejection in your life, do this to conquer it: (1) Stop defining yourself by your circumstances or physical appearance. (2) Focus on who God says you are in His Word. (3) Don't allow negative criticism to enter your heart. (4) Don't surrender to failure. Keep trying; you will win! (5) Keep meditating on how much the Father loves you and calls you His child.

Let us pray

1. *Father, thank You because You love and value me above all, in Jesus' name.*
2. *Father, forgive me for accommodating wrong thoughts and ideas about myself, in Jesus' name.*
3. *Father, I reject every image in my soul about me that is not from Your Word, in Jesus' name.*
4. *Father, help me to focus on Your love. Fill me with Your love, in Jesus' name.*
5. *Father, I forgive all those who have hurt me and let go of everything I hold against them. Heal my heart, in Jesus' name.*
6. *Father, I command the spirit of rejection tormenting my mind to leave me completely now, by fire, in Jesus' name.*

Sunday 22 June

DON'T BE BITTER; PRAISE!

Read: Psalm 50:10-15

> **Bible in 1 year:** James 1-2
> **Bible in 2 years:** Prov. 23-24

"Offer to God thanksgiving, And pay your vows to the Most High. Call upon Me in the day of trouble; I will deliver you, and you shall glorify Me" (Psalm 50:14-15).

Thanksgiving is God's strategy to express our joy to Him. You cannot know how someone feels until they express it. Every time you thank God, you demonstrate your love and appreciation to God.

Thanksgiving sacrifices include singing praises to God, testifying about what He has done, praying and adoring Him, and presenting thanksgiving offerings to Him, especially during times of trial. Our heavenly Father expects us to continually celebrate Him, regardless of what we are going through. *"Therefore, by Him let us continually offer the sacrifice of praise to God, that is, the fruit of our lips, giving thanks to His name" (Hebrews 13:15).* Peter emphasizes this too, *"But you are a chosen generation, a royal priesthood, a holy nation, His own special people, THAT YOU MAY PROCLAIM THE PRAISES OF HIM who called you out of darkness into His marvelous light" (1 Peter 2:9).*

Child of God, don't fail in performing this spiritual duty daily. Regrettably, some Christians, instead of serving as "Kingdom praise givers," have become "Kingdom complainers." They are bitter against God, everyone else, and even themselves, for one reason or another.

In verses 10-13 of our text, God points out clearly that He lacks nothing. If he needed food, He would not ask from you because your resources are too limited to feed Him. Just think about this: How big is God's stomach? If He needed worship, He has trillions of holy angels in heaven to worship Him. The number of angels John saw worshipping God in Revelation 5:11 was enormous – 100.000.000.000.000. He is self-sufficient and cannot beg anything from any human being. He can do without you, but you cannot do without him.

So, where then is the place of your thanksgiving sacrifices if God has all He needs? He says, *"Offer to God thanksgiving, And pay your vows to the Most High. Call upon Me in the day of trouble; I will deliver you, and you shall glorify Me" (Psalm 50:14-15).* Your thanksgiving connects you to God's unlimited blessings. So, if you want to experience quick divine interventions, learn to humble yourself and thank God, and avoid bitterness. Learn to thank Him with an offering.

Let us pray
1. *Father, thank You because You cannot abandon me in the day of trouble.*
2. *My Father, forgive me for not celebrating You enough for all that You have done in my life.*
3. *Lord, teach me how to thank You continuously for all Your wonders in our lives.*
4. *I reject the spirit of complaining and welcome the anointing of thanksgiving in Jesus' name.*

5. *My Father, open my eyes to see Your greatness and Your all-sufficiency and teach me to trust You for the supply of all my needs.*

6. *Father, release a special anointing of generosity and love in my heart and the hearts of other Christians, in Jesus' name.*

Read: Acts 13:1-4

> **Bible in 1 year:** Jam. 3-5
> **Bible in 2 years:** Prov. 25-26

"Your ears shall hear a word behind you, saying, 'This is the way, walk in it," Whenever you turn to the right hand Or whenever you turn to the left" (Isaiah 30:21).

Y ou can't hear until you listen! Friend, you will never know God's voice until you start practicing listening in the place of prayer. Your prayer altar is supposed to be a place where you have intimate communion with the Holy Spirit and receive divine guidance as you listen to His voice. Hence, your prayer time should not be a monologue but a dialogue with your creator. In Isaiah 1:18, He says, *"Come now, and let us reason together,' Says the LORD" (Isaiah 1:18).* He didn't say, "Come and throw words at me and leave."

Unfortunately, many pray without concrete results because they pray with closed ears. The Father says, "Come let us reason together." In other words, bring your situation and let's think together on how to resolve it. Dear friend, it will take you and God thinking together to change your condition. Never throw your responsibility at Him. He can never do what you are supposed to do. You are transferring your responsibilities to God when you pray like a CD player and do not listen to God's voice.

Do you know that prayer gives you access to God's mind? God told Jeremiah, *"Call to Me, and I will answer you, and show you great and mighty things, which you do not know" (Jeremiah 33:3).* You can actually tap into the mind, will, purpose, and wisdom of God concerning your destiny in the place of prayer. In prayer, there is an exchange of thoughts. You share with God what is on your mind, and He shares with you what is on His mind. The result is that your mind becomes saturated with divine ideas and thoughts. You gain divine revelation, insight, and guidance. This is the secret behind the strength of all successful people in God's kingdom.

Barnabas and Saul stepped out into the Mission field boldly because they heard directly from God in the place of prayer. Whenever you go to pray, always listen to the voice of the Holy Spirit. He will speak to you.

Let us pray

1. *Father, thank You for the anointing of divine revelation activated on me by this Word.*
2. *Father, cleanse my spiritual eyes of anything that blurs my vision and hearing, in Jesus' name.*
3. *Father, help me not to miss Your will concerning any area of my life this season, in Jesus' name.*
4. *Dear Holy Spirit, cause that my mind should be connected to the mind of God at all times.*
5. *I command every satanic network interfering with my destiny to catch fire now, in Jesus' name.*
6. *O Lord, restore the spirit of revelation mightily in the church in this land, in Jesus' name.*

Prophetic Prayers of the Week

1. *Father, thank You because You will cause the enemies of my soul to fall in the pit they have dug for me, in Jesus' name.*

2. *Every appointment arranged for me with premature death by the kingdom of darkness is aborted by the blood of Jesus, in Jesus' name.*

3. *Every ancestral covenant claiming anything from me is erased by the blood of Jesus, in Jesus' name.*

Tuesday 24 June   **DON'T PROVOKE GOD**

Read: 1 Kings 16:1-13

> **Bible in 1 year:** Gal. 1-3
> **Bible in 2 years:** Prov. 27-28

"Do not be deceived, God is not mocked; for whatever a man sows, that he will also reap" (Galatians 6:7).

Sincere worship and generosity produce blessings; sin induces calamity. *"The one who sows to please his sinful nature, from that nature will reap destruction; the one who sows to please the Spirit, from the Spirit will reap eternal life" (Galatians 6:8 NIV).* Do you know that you are sowing seeds of provocation anytime you break God's commandments? Seeds of provocation attract destruction. Some people's adversity is caused by carnality, immorality, vanity, and idolatry.

King Baasha of Israel provoked God's anger through his idolatry and perversity (vs. 7). His iniquity angered God, triggering transgenerational calamities in his household. Zimri, one of his generals, assassinated him alongside all his sons. This fulfilled God's prophetic Word declared to him by Prophet Jehu (1 Kings 16:1-7).

Today, some people have become too familiar with God that they take Him for granted. They think they can do just anything in the name of Jesus. Such people pronounce false prophecies when God has not spoken. They pollute themselves with immorality but still stand before God's people to minister. Others use God's name to dupe people of their hard-earned money. Worst of all, some use occult powers to carry out ministry in God's house. All these evil practices provoke God, and He will judge them.

Today, God is warning us through this Word. Don't provoke Him! The consequences will be terrible. However, the good news is that it doesn't matter how far you have fallen; God can restore you if you sincerely repent and amend your ways. Beloved, put your life in order so that God's hand of favor can rest on your life.

Let us pray

1. *Father, thank You for today and this warning message to us.*
2. *Examine your life before God and identify those things you do that provoke God. Ask God to forgive and cleanse you with the blood of Jesus Christ.*
3. *Rededicate your whole life to Him today and commit yourself to walk in His ways.*

   Lay your hand on your head and pray:

4. *I command any evil anointing on my life to dry off now, in Jesus' name.*
5. *Let the mantle of fire for cleansing and restoration fall on my life now, in Jesus' name.*
6. *O Lord, release the river of righteousness to purge our pulpits of every falsehood.*

Wednesday 25 June   **SUBMIT TO ONE ANOTHER**

Read: Ephesians 5:21-33

> **Bible in 1 year:** Gal. 4-6
> **Bible in 2 years:** Prov. 29-30

"Submit to one another out of reverence for Christ"
(Ephesians 5:21).

Mutual submission is vital for building healthy relationships. Any time we disrespect or abuse authority, we poison our relationships. We cannot relate well with one another when we don't value, appreciate, and respect ourselves.

The word "Submit" in our main verse is the Greek *"Hupotasso,"* which means: (1) To yield or submit to someone's authority or leadership voluntarily. (2) Mutual respect, humility, and a willingness to serve one another. (3) Not coercive. The word does not convey a sense of coercion or forced submission, but rather a voluntary and loving response. Paul's call to submission in Ephesians 5:21 refers to mutual submission among believers. He emphasizes that every believer ought to have a servant-like attitude towards one another. As God's children, we must prioritize others' needs over our own. In the context of marriage, the verses instruct wives to submit to their husbands, just as the Church submits to Christ.

Today, most people don't like the phrase, "Submit to one another." The independent spirit that characterizes today's society conflicts with the idea of being subject to other people. Rejecting the idea of submitting to one another leaves the family, the church, and the society in chaos.

A wife who loves her husband will submit to him, respect him, and accept his leadership. You cannot claim to love him if you don't respect him. In premarital counseling, we tell the young ladies, "Don't marry a man you cannot respect."

The husband, as the leader of the family, is supposed to guide, guard, and govern his home with Christlike love. You cannot build a healthy marriage without sacrificial love. If you love your wife, you will value, appreciate, and provide for her. You won't abuse her. Back in the 1800s, a husband in a village in Pennsylvania was beating his wife. The other men in the village decided to take action. One man wrote: "A bunch of us men went over there and took all of his clothes off and drug him through a field of thistles backwards. Then we told him that if he continued to deal unkindly with his wife, we would not take it very lightly. We were going to get upset next time."

Should the men or women in the community intervene in your home to force you to fulfill your marital responsibilities? No!

Let us pray

1. *Father, thank You for making me a prince/princess in Your Kingdom, in Jesus' name.*
2. *Father, set me free from rebellion and every form of insubordination in my relationships, in Jesus' name.*
3. *I receive the grace to submit to authority and respect and value others according to God's will, in Jesus' name.*

4. *Are you married? Pray for grace to love your wife as Christ. Ask for grace to submit to your husband like the Church does to Christ.*
5. *Pray for some marriages you know that are having crises.*
6. *Pray for your children that they would respect authority.*

Thursday 26 June **HE IS FAITHFUL TO FORGIVE**

Read: Luke 15:17-20

> **Bible in 1 year:** Isa. 1-3
> **Bible in 2 years:** Prov. 31; Eccl. 1

"If we confess our sins, he is faithful and just and will forgive us our sins and purify us from all unrighteousness" (1 John 1:9).

There is no ugly sin God cannot forgive. He can forgive you if you sincerely repent, no matter what you have done. Do you need forgiveness today? God is faithful and just enough to forgive and cleanse you no matter what you have done. Return to Him with all your heart.

1 John 1:9 is God's promise to Christian who have a relationship with Jesus Christ. God wants to bless us and answer our prayers, so He tells us to deal with our sins, which can hinder us. We need to accept Christ's sacrifice and repent of our wrongdoing. We need to uproot every secret sin and disobedience in our lives to pray effectively.

Our sins are forgiven when we go to Christ, who cleanses and covers us with His blood. We need continual cleansing so that we can live before God in holiness—the holiness Christ died to provide. God is saying, "If you want Me to do business with you, you have to get rid of sin and disobedience." Why? Sin separates us from God. *"But your iniquities have separated you from your God; your sins have hidden his face from you, so that he will not hear" (Isaiah 59:2).*

Friend, you don't need to go around bearing guilt for sinning. You should rather boldly go to God and ask for forgiveness and receive cleansing. God is compassionate and gracious, and He will forgive you.

God can also deal with the sins you have committed unconsciously. King David prayed, *"Who can discern his errors? Forgive my hidden faults"* (Psalm 19:12). We also have this promise from God's Word: *"For as high as the heavens are above the earth, so great is his love for those who fear him; as far as the east is from the west, so far has he removed our transgressions from us* (Psalm 103:11–12).

Let us pray

1. *Father, thank You because there is no sin You cannot forgive, in Jesus' name.*
2. *Are there issues you want God to forgive and liberate you from? Present them to Him now and ask for forgiveness.*
3. *Father, I receive the blood of Jesus Christ as a deep cleansing agent in my life, in Jesus' name.*
4. *Place your hand on your belly and pray 5 times, "Fire of God, fall now and purge me of every root of iniquity, in Jesus' name."*
5. *I command the throne of the enemy on any area of my life to catch fire and burn to ashes, in Jesus' name.*
6. *Father, vaccinate my soul and spirit with the fire of holiness, in Jesus' name.*

Friday 27 June   **USE YOUR**
                     COVENANT RIGHT

Read: Hebrews 4:14-16

> **Bible in 1 year:** Isa. 4-6
> **Bible in 2 years:** Eccl. 2-3

"But as many as received him, to them gave he power to become the sons of God, even to them that believe on his name" (John 1:12).

You cannot do any legal business with God if you are not in a proper relationship with Him through Christ. Jesus cancelled our sins with His sacrifice on the cross, providing us with forgiveness and legal access to God through His name. Only the children of God can claim power through Jesus' name. John 1:12 says, *"But as many as received him, to them gave he power to become the sons of God, even to them that believe on his name."* Are you among the many who have received Him and believed in His name?

Friend, the authority we have in Jesus' name through prayer is based on our covenant relationship with God through Christ. *"But the ministry Jesus has received is as superior to theirs [the priests of Israel] as the covenant of which he is mediator is superior to the old one, and it is founded on better promises" (Hebrews 8:6).* We can pray directly to God in Jesus' name because Jesus has given us authority to do so.

In the New Testament, Jesus made seven statements, such as the following, authorizing us to use His name in prayer to God: *"I tell you the truth, my Father will give you whatever you ask in my name." Until now, you have not asked for anything in my name. Ask, and you will receive, and your joy will be complete. Though I have been speaking figuratively, a time is coming when I will no longer use this kind of language but will tell you plainly about my Father. In that day you will ask in my name" (John 16:23–26).*

Have you received Jesus Christ as your Lord and Savior, and are you living as His disciple? Don't forget your covenant right to use His name. Once you have a driver's license, you can drive your car on the highway without fear. Use Jesus' name boldly to confront the devil and enforce divine order in your life and family.

Let us pray
1. *Father, thank You for giving me the right to use Jesus' name.*
2. *Father, shine Your light in my heart and cause me to understand Your will concerning my life as a covenant child in the Kingdom.*
3. *Father, let Your mighty hand move in my life and establish order, in Jesus' name.*
4. *I command darkness to leave my ministry, health, marriage, and finances, in Jesus' name.*
5. *Father, let many who come across me this year see Your glory and turn to Jesus Christ, in Jesus' name.*
6. *Father, baptize me with Your Spirit and use me to answer someone's complex question this season, in Jesus' name.*

GOVERN YOUR
                        TONGUE

Read: Proverbs 23:15-16

> **Bible in 1 year:** Isa. 7-9
> **Bible in 2 years:** Eccl. 4-5

"Whoever guards his mouth and tongue Keeps his soul from troubles" (Proverbs 21:23).

Your tongue has tremendous power to raise or erase you. The negative things (Curses) you pronounce on your children in anger can wipe out your family. You can study the impact of Jacob's curses on his three sons: Reuben, Simeon, and Levi. Their offspring faced lots of problems.

History has it that only one man in American history has ever resigned from the presidency – Richard Nixon. What pushed him to it? Some sources say it was the tapes of his private conversations. As Bob Gass says, "It wasn't the tapes, it was his tongue." The tapes only carried what he said. So, his tongue terminated his stay in the White House? How many relationships, marriages, and organizations have been destroyed by the tongue?

Our main verse is a counsel: *"Whoever guards his mouth and tongue Keeps his soul from troubles" (Proverbs 21:23).* If you cannot guard your tongue, which is a two-edged sword, it will slay others and ruin you too. The words "Tongue, mouth, and lips" are mentioned about 150 times in the book of Proverbs. This emphasizes that we must be mindful of what comes out of our mouths or face the consequences.

It is said that in fifty years, the average person can say enough words to create twelve thousand volumes of three hundred pages each. If this is true, then think about the content of your books, assuming that all you say was written down. The sad truth is that some negative things you say will never be forgotten.

In our text, God, through Solomon's words, wants us to be wise. He is saying, "*My son [my daughter], if your heart is wise, then my heart will be glad indeed; my inmost being will rejoice when your lips speak what is right*" *(vvs. 15-16 NIV).*
Choose the way of wisdom, which is checking the things you say.

Let us pray

1. *Father, thank You because You gave me a tongue to be a blessing, not a curse.*
2. *Father, let Your blessing rest on my tongue, in Jesus' name.*
3. *O Lord, teach me to rule my tongue, in Jesus' name.*
4. *Father, guide my feet into the way of peace, in Jesus' name.*
5. *Father, You give strength to the weak; make me unbreakable, in Jesus' name.*
6. *Father, silence the tongue of the wicked raised against me, in Jesus' name.*

Sunday 29 June   **CHOOSE TO PLEASE GOD**

Read: 1 Peter 2:20-23

Bible in 1 year: Isa. 10-12
Bible in 2 years: Eccl. 6-7

"When a man's ways please the LORD, He makes even his enemies to be at peace with him" (Proverbs 16:7).

Dear friend, pleasing God should not be a difficult task if you choose to relate to Him in absolute obedience to His commands and total trust in His sovereign power. *"For God is working in you, giving you the desire and the power to do what pleases him" (Philippians 2:13).* This verse implies that you can please God if you are willing to do so.

Jesus Christ remains our perfect example in the school of pleasing God. As 1 Peter 2:20-23 states about Him, *"If you suffer for doing good and endure it patiently, God is pleased with you. For God called you to do good, even if it means suffering, just as Christ suffered for you. He is your example, and you must follow in His steps. He never sinned, nor ever deceived anyone. He did not retaliate when He was insulted, nor threaten revenge when He suffered. He left His case in the hands of God, who always judges fairly" (NLT).* If you desire to please God, follow Jesus' example!

Pleasing God is a choice you have to make daily. Here is the story of a man who chose to please God daily: "A man purchased a newspaper at a news stand every day. He always greeted the vendor very courteously, but in return received very irritable and insolent treatment; the vendor would rudely shove the newspaper in his face. The man, however, would politely smile and wish him a nice day. This went on for several days until a friend asked, "Does he always treat you this rudely?" The man replied, "Unfortunately, he does." The friend asked further, "Are you always so polite and friendly to him?" The man replied, "Yes, I am." The friend continued, "Why are you so nice to him when he is so rude to you?" The man replied, "Because I don't want him to decide how I will act."

Any time you choose to please God instead of pleasing yourself, you give Him the opportunity to manifest His glory to your world.

Let us pray
1. *Merciful and Everlasting Father, thank You for giving me a perfect example to follow – Jesus Christ.*
2. *Father, help me to live as the light of the world and the salt of the earth among the ungodly, in Jesus' name.*
3. *Father, fill my heart with wisdom to deal with the ungodly, in Jesus' name.*
4. *Father, fill me with the desire and the wisdom I need to please You in everything I do, in Jesus' name.*
5. *Father, let good always triumph over evil in my life, wherever I go, in Jesus' name.*
6. *Pray for those who are suffering in this nation because of their faith; that they will not falter, in Jesus' name.*

Monday 30 June   **PRAY FOR**
                            CAMEROON

Read: Nehemiah 9:26-28

> **Bible in 1 year:** Isa. 13-15
> **Bible in 2 years:** (Catch-up)

"Righteousness exalts a nation, but sin is a reproach"
(Proverbs 14:34).

A nation is raised or ruined by the acts of its citizens towards God or fellow man. When crime, corruption, and a carefree lifestyle are unchecked among people, they begin to devour themselves. Currently, amid the Anglophone crisis, kidnapping, rape, murder, and assassination have become part of the daily lives of the people of the North West and South West Regions of Cameroon.

God, our Creator, is merciful and compassionate and will not be silent forever. Our text summarizes how he intervened on several occasions to rescue Israel from their pain. How did He do it? He raised men and women with a heart for the people to labor for a change. He will raise among us an order of leaders who will take the bull by the horns and bring the needed order.

As you pray for divine intervention in Cameroon, know that there are three types of people the devil is using to ruin our nation and three types of people God will use to raise the nation:

1. **Three types of persons Satan is using to ruin Cameroon:**
   a) Those whom God has empowered to solve our problems but are not ready to take any action. If a fire is razing a neighbor's house, and you have water to quench it, but for any reason, you stay quiet; you are part of the problem.
   b) Those who are sponsoring wickedness. Evil men are sponsoring some young men to commit heinous crimes. They benefit while the people lament.
   c) Those who go to Satan for powers to run politics, business, ministry, etc. They are polluting the land with demonic spirits.

We must pray that God will lead them to repentance or replace them with people who will bless the nation.

2. **Three types of persons God will use to raise Cameroon:**
   a) People with a deep love for the nation – patriotic citizens (Romans 9:1-3; Nehemiah 1:1-10)
   b) People in leadership who hate evil and corruption. God will use them to impose changes.
   c) People who love and trust God with all their hearts. Change is war, and it takes people with lion courage to raise a great nation.

Pray for Cameroon according to Proverbs 28:12, *"When the [uncompromisingly] righteous triumph, there is great glory and celebration; but when the wicked rise [to power], men hide.*

Let us pray
1. *Father, thank You for Your love and great plans for this nation.*

2. *Father, be merciful for our rebellion against You and come to our rescue.*
3. *Father, let the enemies of Cameroon decrease in power, while nation-builders should increase, in Jesus' name.*
4. *Father, raise instruments to solve the Anglophone crisis perfectly.*
5. *Fire of God, fall in the high and lower places of this nation and judge the works of witchcraft and occultism, in Jesus' name.*
6. *Father, release the Spirit of revival in the churches and stir a change that will affect the entire nation.*

Prophetic Prayers of the Week

1. *Father, I thank You because You have terminated destruction in my life by the blood of Jesus Christ.*
2. *Every poison of sickness working in my body is neutralized by the blood of Jesus, in Jesus' name.*
3. *In the name of Jesus, I declare that the grace of God is sufficient for me. As such, nothing shall quench my faith, and obstacles will serve as stepping stones for me this month.*

WHAT YOUR SUPPORT WILL DO

It is very clear through the numerous miracles, breakthroughs and transformation of lives that God has chosen to use this ministry to stir a revival among His people in Cameroon and beyond. I received the call alone but I cannot execute it alone. You have a unique role to play in this divine project. Join us as we take the Gospel to every corner of Cameroon and beyond.

We want to start placing copies of this book in hotels, hospitals, schools and homes, to touch the lives of people with the gospel of Jesus Christ. Just as you have been blessed by this book, they too will be mightily blessed.

TESTIMONY

Every month, hundreds of copies of this Prayer Storm Daily Prayer Guide are distributed freely, thanks to the kind gesture of our partners. May God bless all of you who faithfully sponsor this outreach through your financial seed. You too can sponsor 10, 25, 50, 100 or even more copies to be printed and distributed charge-free to those who are hungry for the word.

Call the numbers: (237) 699.90.26.18 or 674.49.58.95 send an email to voiceofrevivalcameroon@yahoo.com.
If you want to become a distributor of our literature, contact us directly and we will give you the directives on how to do so.

WHERE TO BUY THIS PRAYER GUIDE

CRN Centres

- **Yaounde:** *Prayer Storm Headquarters*, **Biyem-Assi Carrefour,** opposite Campus Crusade for Christ: 681.72.24.04/ 696.56.58.64
- **Bamenda:** Revival Christian Book Center, **Cow Street**: 675.14.04.50/ 694.20.04.51
- **Douala/PK 8:** All American Depot opposite Lycée **Cité des Palmiers**: 678.04.11.41/ 696.90.76.09/ 670.34.42.32

Adamawa

- **Banyo:** FGM: 677.92.05.98/ 674.64.71.31
- **Meinganga:** EEL: 699.65.02.67/ 652.70.40.68
- **Ngaoundere:** EEC Mont des Oliviers: 674.14.20.51, EEL: 690.06.37.14
- **Tibati:** EEC: 681.01.33.34

Centre

- **Eseka:** FGM: 675.07.56.24
- **Mbalmayo:** EEC: 675.12.86.85/
- **Mfou:** FGM: 677.36.43.28
- **Monatelé:** FGM: 677.58.42.99
- **Yaounde:** EEC **Biyem-assi**: 675.61.86.00/ 677.49.95.83/ 691.26.18.08, EEC **Nlongkak**: 677.56.41.09, EEC **Nouvelle Alliance**: 670.80.56.93, FGM **Biyem-assi**: 675.14.72.70, FGM **Etoug-Ebé**: 671.47.75.78/ 673.50.42.33, Galaxy Computers, Châteaux **Ngoa-Ekelle**: 670.52.75.26, **Yaounde: Librairie Chrétienne** Les Champions op. Total Caveau, **Mvog-Ada**: 675.51.02.86, **LC Maison de la Grâce**, Montée Jouvence op. Olympia:

675.38.46.96, **LC Maison de la Bénédiction**, Marché Nsam: 691.64.47.84, **LC la Rhema**, Marché Essos, Terminus: 679.39.37.42, **LC Maison du Salut**, Pharmacie du Soleil, Carrefour MEEC: 674.85.16.33/ 699.33.85.11, **LC Livre de Vie**, Mini ferme: 675.00.45.60, **LC Bethesda**, Tsinga: 679.97.06.26, **Overcomers Christian Bookshop**, op. Djongolo Hospital, EtoaMeki: 677.16.46.20, **Mount Zion Christian Bookshop**, op. SONEL TKC: 663.25.86.23 / 675.21.94.35, **Tongolo**: 675.62.86.00, **Olembe**: 651.63.52.34, **DGI-Carrefour Abbia** 652.22.22.49, **Messassi**: 675.24.70.73, **Nkozoa**: 670.29.50.18, **Essos**: 677.53.94.52, **Odzja**: 679.97.47.08, **Etoug-Ebé**: 675.37.18.11, **Mimboman**: 699.90.52.84, **Poste Centrale**: 650.70.08.07, **Emombo**: 699.90.52.84, **Lycée Emana**: 677.86.23.14

East
- **Batouri:** FGM: 664.86.41.80
- **Bertoua:** CBC, **quartier Ngaikada** ou **Aprilé centrale** sous-préfecture: 678.00.63.20/ 694.25.69.20, Collège Bilingue de l'Orient, entrée Hôpital Régionale, **quartier Italy**: 670.56.81.49, FGM, **Nkolbikon**: 696.57.95.43, 677.65.46.76, FGM, **Tigaza**: 674.15.13.18
- **Yokadouma:** FGM: 673.16.24.95/ 696.51.73.70

Far-North
- **Maroua:** Église Missionnaire du Réveil (EMIR) **Baoliwop**: 694.43.33.63, FGM **Harde**: 675.33.12.27, Roman Catholic Church: 673.15.19.76
- **Yagoua:** FGM: 675.691.869

Littoral

Douala: Dakar: La Gloire Phone, immeuble X Tigi, Commissariat 11e: 697.60.57.85, **Kotto:** Behind Neptune fuel station, **Bloc M:** 677.68.18.52, **Bonaberi:** 677.89.87.46, **Akwa:** 691.04.14.59/ 677.91.29.45, **Logpom:** 677.68.18.52/ 651.78.57.30**, Carrefour Lycée de Maképé:** 698.09.42.63, **PK 12 (Marché):** 677.91.29.45/ 696.13.99.26, **Texaco-Nkoulouluon:** 675.18.79.85/695112610 691.04.14.59, **Terminus Saint Michel :** 675187985, La Gloire Phone, Maison X. Tigi, **Carrefour entrée Bille:** 678.19.90.85, **PK 21:** 670.79.05.40/ 691.04.14.59, **Bonanjo:** 691.04.14.59, 677061705 691.04.14.59, **Ange Raphael ESSEC:** 694.26.12.28/ 677.91.29.45, 698360441, **Bonamoussadi Maetur:** 694.26.12.28/ 677.91.29.45, **Village:** 670.79.05.40/ 691.04.14.5, Sure Foundation **Bonabéri:** Ancienne route op. Lycée de Bonaberi Winners Chapel: 671.403.761

- **Nkongsamba:** FGM: 676.40.90.55
- **Melong - GCEPAL:** Tel: 677.80.16.45

North

- **Garoua:** FGM: 678.67.04.22/ 699.91.91.65

North-West

- **Bamenda:** Bamenda Main Market, **Shed 15**: 679.45.11.88, Carmel Cooperative Credit Union (CarCCUL), **Sonac Street**/Tél: 651.04.21.27, FGM NW1 Area office, opposite Garanti Express: 679.46.63.31, FGM, **Cow Street**: 677.21.97.22, FGM, **Mbomassa**: 683.40.40.88, Omega Fire Ministry, **Foncha junction**: 677.93.19.98, ACADI head office, **Wakiki junction**: 672.82.77.84, SUMAN Christian Book Center, **Sonac Street**:

675.72.91.32/ 665.49.98.48, Victory Computers, Food market, **Fishpond hill**: 677.64.19.54, Wailing Women: 696.00.35.07/ 674.57.36.76

- **Batibo:** FGM: 677.31.25.45
- **Njinikom/Mbingo:** BERUDA: 677.60.14.07
- **Jakiri:** FGM, **Nkar**: 677.73.82.91
- **Kumbo:** FGM: 675.72.91.32
- **Mbengwi:** FGM: 677.33.73.86
- **Ndop:** Bruno Bijouterie, Central park: 674.97.59.34
- **Wum:** FGM Central Town: 677.64.32.56, PCC Kesu: 677.13.83.51

<u>West</u>
- **Bafang:** FGM, **Bafang**: 655.00.25.57
- **Bafia:** FGM: 675.21.92.95/ 695.54.96.14
- **Bafoussam:** Alliance biblique du Cameroun, **Tamdja**, SOREPCO: 699.74.79.10, Radio Bonne Nouvelle: 699.93.09.32, Librairie chrétienne du **Camp** oignon: 699.51.47.25, LC PAROLE DE VIE, **gare routière de** Ndiangdam: 699.75.50.99, Dépôt RAYON AMBIANCE **marché A**: 699.42.78.47, EEC **Tamdja**: 696.14.90.16, EEC **Kamkop**: 699.44.03.59, EEC **Plateau**: 696.17.54.23, EEC **Toket**: 695.56.43.61, EEC **SOCADA**: 697.85.65.65, EEC **Tyo-Baleng**: 670.89.70.52, EEC **Kouogouo**: 675.42.27.86, EEC **Diangdam**: 698.35.20.37, FGM **Kamkop**: 653.83.11.80, Faith Bible Church: 683.94.01.21
- **Baham:** FGM: 677.47.55.79
- **Bandjoun:** FGM: 676.41.49.09
- **Bangangte:** EEC **Banekane**: 677.86.47.68
- **Banyo:** FGM: 677.92.05.98/ 674.64.71.31

- **Dschang:** FGM: 675.18.79.85/ 656.20.07.02, FGM **Minmeto**: 681.08.78.37/ 655.01.81.09
- **Foumban:** Décoration Splendeur, **CAMOCO**/Tel.: 677.79.30.83/ 694.85.09.25
- **Kombou:** EEC: 675.81.36.07
- **Mbouda:** FGM: 696.10.41.33/ 676.36.18.11, Cyber Café Pressing near Espace Saint Pierre du Fossie, op. Party House: 675.00.91.15, EEC **Mbouda Centre**: 695.61.97.79

South
- **Ebolowa:** FGM: 677.66.00.19/ 671.90.97.22
- **Kribi:** Carrefour Django: 675.957.912
- **Kye-Ossi:** FGM: 678.78.00.90/ 699.95.96.99

South-West
- **Buea:** FGM **Molyko**: 677.86.47.68, Molyko, near Express Union, **Check Point**: 675.06.37.78,
- **Ekona:** FGM: 675.84.26.91
- **Kumba:** Caisse Populaire Coopérative Carmel (CarCCUL), **Sonac Street**: 675.45.12.21, Glorious Christian Book Center, **Sonac Street**: 677.62.58.49
- **Lebialem:** FGM de **Talung**, Bamumbu – Wabane: 670.466.121
- **Limbe:** Librairie Amen, **New town**: 677.16.51.62, FGM **Mawoh**: 675.78.94.19, FGM **Cow Fence**: 675.73.20.02
- **Misaje:** Kingdom Restoration Parish (KRP) **opposite the hospital**: 679.33.66.53
- **Mutengene:** FGM: 675.36.36.84
- **Muyuka:** FGM: 673.428.985, Royal Priesthood Nursery and Primary School: 677.72.76.80

- **Tiko:** FGM: 654.88.75.57, 674.47.34.36
- **Tombel:** Baptist Church Waterfall: 677.92.33.58

ABROAD:

- **N'Djamena (Chad):** Evang. Kaltouma Aguidi: (235) 95.01.99.92
- **Libreville (Gabon):** Rev. Petipa Flaubert: (241) 05.31.27.39

Pay for your book orders (DISTRIBUTORS ONLY) at:
EcoBank, Acc. No: 0200212620638901 **or** ORANGE
Mobile Money, Acc. No: 696880058
Info lines: (237) 677436964, 675686005, 673571953, 679465717;
crnprayerstorm@gmail.com,
prayerstorm@christianrestorationnetwork.org,
www.christianrestorationnetwork.org

Send Financial Support to: ECOBANK Bamenda Acc.
No: 0040812604565101 **or** Carmel Cooperative Credit
Union Ltd. Bamenda Acc. No: 261 **or** ORANGE Mobile
Money: 699902618 **or** MTN Mobile Money: 674495895.

PUBLICATIONS BY CHRISTIAN RESTORATION NETWORK (CRN/PRAYER STORM)

1- Prayer Storm Daily Prayer Guide (monthly devotional)
2- Power Must Change Hands Vol.1: Dealing with Evil Foundations
3- Power Must Change Hands Vol.2: Pursue Overtake and Recover All
4- Power Must Change Hands Vol.3: Jesus Christ Must Reign
5- Power Must Change Hands Vol.4: Arise and Shine
6- Power Must Change Hands Vol.5: Family Restoration 1
7- Power Must Change Hands Vol.6: Family Restoration 2
8- Power Must Change Hands Vol.7: Raise an Altar
9- Power Must Change Hands Vol.8: Commanding Total Victory
10- Power Must Change Hands Vol.9: Enjoying Your Freedom in Christ
11- Power Must Change Hands Vol.10: Supernatural Breakthrough
12- Festival of Fire Series No.1: Let the Fire Fall
13- Festival of Fire Series No.2: Anointed Vessels
14- Festival of Fire Series No.3: God's Agent of Revival
15- Festival of Fire Series No.4: Raising Altars of Restoration
16- Dominion
17- Divine Overflow
18- Unbreakable
19- Higher Heights

NB: Our publications are in English and French.

For copies, contact your local books store or direct your request to:

Prayer Storm Team
P.O. Box 5018 Nkwen, Bamenda
Tel.: (237) 679465717 or 675686005 or 677436964
crnprayerstorm@gmail.com
prayerstorm@christianrestorationnetwork.org

Prayer Storm Online Store:

With MTN or Orange Mobile Money *(for those in Cameroon)* and E-Wallet *(for those abroad)*, you can easily obtain the electronic version of this book and other CRN publications via **www.amazon.com** or via **www.amazon.com** at

https://shorturl.at/pqxyT or
www.christianrestorationnetwork.org/our-bookstore.
https://goo.gl/ktf3rT

Contact (237) 679.46.57.17 or
prayerstorm@christianrestorationnetwork.org

www.ingramcontent.com/pod-product-compliance
Lightning Source LLC
Chambersburg PA
CBHW072006090426
42740CB00011B/2109